What Is a Superhero?

What Is a Superhero?

Edited By Robin S. Rosenberg and Peter Coogan

OXFORD
UNIVERSITY PRESS

OXFORD
UNIVERSITY PRESS

Oxford University Press is a department of the University of Oxford.
It furthers the University's objective of excellence in research, scholarship,
and education by publishing worldwide.

Oxford   New York Auckland   Cape Town   Dar es Salaam   Hong Kong   Karachi
Kuala Lumpur   Madrid   Melbourne   Mexico City   Nairobi
New Delhi   Shanghai   Taipei   Toronto

With offices in
Argentina   Austria   Brazil   Chile   Czech Republic   France   Greece
Guatemala   Hungary   Italy   Japan   Poland   Portugal   Singapore
South Korea   Switzerland   Thailand   Turkey   Ukraine   Vietnam

Oxford is a registered trademark of Oxford University Press in the
UK and certain other countries.

Published in the United States of America by
Oxford University Press 198
Madison Avenue, New York, NY 10016

Library of Congress Cataloging-in-Publication Data
What is a superhero?/edited by Robin S. Rosenberg and Peter Coogan.
pages cm
ISBN 978–0–19–979527–7 (acid-free paper)
1. Superheroes.   2. Comic books, strips, etc.
I. Rosenberg, Robin S., editor of compilation. II. Coogan,
Peter M. (Peter MacFarland), editor of compilation.
PN6714.W48 2013
741.5'9—dc23   2013000761

1 3 5 7 9 8 6 4 2
Printed in the United States of America
on acid-free paper

Contents

Foreword

Michael Uslan is just about the ideal person to introduce a collection of essays on the definition of the superhero. He is both scholar and creator. He taught the first accredited college course on comics, at Indiana University, and wrote the first textbook on comics. His passion for *Batman* comics led him to envision a dark version of Batman for the big screen. Uslan became the originator and Executive Producer of all the *Batman* movies from Tim Burton's 1989 *Batman* through 2012's *The Dark Knight Rises*. As if that weren't enough, he also writes comic books, including Batman, and has recently authored his memoir, *The Boy Who Loved Batman*. In 2012, Uslan received the world's first ever Doctorate in Comic Books.

Heroes and villains have been essential parts of folklore and mythology since the beginnings of oral traditions and storytelling. Across the millennia, the heroes have come in many forms and sizes, varying from culture to culture around the world. The villains emerged as sometimes evil and sometimes spiteful and jealous gods, monsters, ogres, wizards, warlocks, witches, kings, knaves, and even as the dark side of the heroes themselves. So, when and how does a hero earn the right to be called or designated as a "superhero"?

Does being a superhero require one or more superpowers? Conversely, is that the same requirement for a supervillain? Thus, does the strength of Hercules or Samson qualify them for membership in some ancient version of a Justice League? Do the powers of Medusa or Circe or Macbeth's three witches entitle them to become part of some legendary Secret Society of Supervillains? On the surface, the answers to the questions we pose seem obvious and simple. When Superman made his debut in June 1938[*] in the pages of *Action Comics* #1 as comicbookdom's first superhero, the requirements of this new class of heroes seemed set in stone: a benevolent Hercules equipped with powers and abilities far beyond those of mortal men; a colorful costume evoking a circus strongman, the man on the flying trapeze, the human cannonball, or a tumbling acrobat; and perhaps also a secret identity as earlier utilized by the Scarlet Pimpernel and Zorro. Yes, it all appeared so very, very simple... until the world's *second* superhero made his debut in May 1939.

The Batman mysteriously appeared in *Detective Comics* #27 and rewrote the rules Superman had set down just 11 months before. He looked like a superhero. He had the colorful costume and cape. He had a secret identity. But he had *no* superpowers. Batman's greatest so-called superpower was possibly his humanity. If the Batman was,

---

[*] Editors' note: *Action Comics* #1 was cover dated June 1938 but actually went on sale a few months beforehand. Because sales records are not easily available, the convention in comics history is to date comic books by their cover dates, rather than their sale dates.

indeed, a superhero as much as Superman, what now would be the qualifying criteria? As the fledgling comic book industry grew and dozens, then hundreds, of these caped crusaders and mystery men made their four-color appearances, the true answer became clearer and clearer.

When young Bruce Wayne watched in abject horror as his parents were gunned down before his eyes, he made a vow...a *vow*. At that frozen moment in time, he made a sacrifice...a *sacrifice*. He sacrificed his childhood on a blood-soaked concrete altar in order to dedicate the rest of his life to getting the evil one who did this...getting all the evil ones...even if it meant having to go through Hell in order to do so. It was a commitment he was willing to make and see through to the end...a *commitment*. In order to accomplish this mission, he had to train relentlessly to become the best a human being could become physically and mentally...to become *the best*. In doing so, he became an urban warrior...an urban legend...a superhero.

Thus, today we have our own real-life superheroes who fill the bill laid down by Superman and Batman. The firefighters, police, and EMTs who rushed to the World Trade Center during and after its attack are superheroes. The man who jumped onto the subway tracks in New York to rescue a person in distress is more than a fast-thinking Good Samaritan flush with adrenalin; he's a superhero. The doctors or nurses rushing to Haiti in the aftermath of a terrible earthquake are superheroes, and the people they help and save and comfort will swear this to you. The soldier heading off to a distant land is our modern-day, dragon-slaying Beowulf. All these individuals would qualify as members in what in olden days might have been called King Arthur's Knights of the Round Table and in contemporary times might be referred to as the Avengers.

Is there any other definition for "superhero"? My own mother and father sacrificed so much to raise my brother and me, and they taught us life's most important lessons in the process, often by example. They are my superheroes. Who are yours?

I've had the pleasure of appearing with Robin Rosenberg and Peter Coogan on celebrated panels at some of the world's biggest comic book conventions, where we have enthusiastically discussed and debated, in front of what are by now thousands of comic book fans, everything from the psychology of supervillains to the essence of superheroes. Their research, writings, and presentations represent some of the most scholarly work being done or ever having been done in the field. Initially afraid that Robin and Pete would be attempting to teach a graduate-level academic seminar at a Comic Con to a room filled with girls dressed as Harley Quinn, boys dressed as the Joker, and an occasional very large, bearded man dressed as Princess Leia, I was relieved and amazed to experience the entertaining and enlightening approach they bring to a subject that attracts such great interest across fans of both genders, all ages, and all cultures.

When the writers and artists of comic books, beginning in the Golden Age of the late 1930s through World War II and the 1940s, created all these characters and stories, they were trying to make a living in hard times. They were not thinking that what they were in the process of doing was creating a legitimate American art form or America's (and eventually the world's) newest mythology. But in addition to the sheer entertainment and escapist fare they provided us with, their greatest gift was the ideal of the modern-day superhero. And yes, it's true: the ancient gods of Egypt, of Greece and Rome, of the Norse, all still exist—only today they wear spandex and capes.

What is a "superhero"? The secrets lie within the pages that follow. Your quest to find the answers begins now...

Michael Uslan
Somewhere inside Mt. Olympus,
Odin's Palace in Asgard,
the JLA's Hall of Justice,
or maybe just the local fire and police station
2013

Acknowledgments

This book would not have been possible without the many comic book, film, and television writers, artists, actors, directors, and other folks who have contributed their own interpretation of what it means to be a superhero. Many thanks to all the "creators" of superheroes. We are extremely grateful in particular to the comic book writers who contributed to this volume (in reverse alphabetical order, since alphabetical order is the most common way to do it and is inherently unfair to folks whose names begin with letters toward the end of the alphabet): Fred van Lente, Joe Quesada, Dennis O'Neil, Ivory Madison, Jeph Loeb, Paul Levitz, Stan Lee, Danny Fingeroth, Tom DeFalco, and Kurt Busiek. We are grateful to Michael Uslan for writing a foreword, and for collaborating with us on Batman panels at San Diego Comic Con.

Thanks also go to the comic book scholars who contributed to this volume for their insightful musings on what makes a superhero, and for their patience. Of course this book also wouldn't have been possible without superhero fans: those of us curious about superheroes—their lives and stories—and who ponder questions such as, just what *is* a superhero?

We are grateful to Oxford University Press for their support. Specifically, thanks to Abby Gross, Purdy, Suzanne Walker, Justyna Zajac, Joan Bossert, and Tracy O'Hara. Thanks also to Catharine Carlin Alexander and Angelique Rondeau for their support in the initial phases of this book (and to Angelique for the penultimate phase as well).

On the personal side, we thank our families for their support and love: Justin, David, Neil, Rebecca, Stephen, Steven, Bunny, and Ed; Karla, Lila, and Lulu.

Introduction

What is a superhero? We—Robin Rosenberg and Peter Coogan—are asking and answering that question with this book. But is a whole book of essays really needed to answer that question? Everyone knows what a superhero is, right? Yet everyone seems to have a different answer. In fact, this book's origin arose from that fact. Robin was meeting with her editors at Oxford University Press regarding another superhero book she was working on, *Our Superheroes, Ourselves* (which, like the book you're reading now, is part of Oxford's Superhero Series, of which Robin is editor). One of the Oxford folks, who was new to the superhero world, asked, "What exactly *is* a superhero?" Everyone else at the meeting—superhero fans all—had a slightly different answer. Robin then realized that asking—and answering—that very question should be part of the Superhero series.

As for Pete, the definition of the superhero has been his hobbyhorse for most of the past two decades. His dissertation, *The Secret Origin of the Superhero: The Emergence of the Superhero in America from Daniel Boone to Batman*, features 54 pages of obsessive examination of all the extant definitions, plus another 18 proposing—and shooting down—candidates for the title of "First Superhero" (and the title goes to…Superman!). But in the years he spent writing his dissertation, he routinely discussed the topic at conferences, comic book conventions, and cocktail parties with faculty, fans, and friends until he settled the issue for himself (see his "dictionary definition" of the superhero in the first essay of this volume). And he made his conclusions available to the world via his book *Superhero: The Secret Origin of a Genre* (MonkeyBrain Books, 2006). So that should have settled things—but astonishingly, shockingly, other people still have their own opinions.

In fact, the question of what a superhero is has become central to our culture's understanding of itself and our future. The superhero genre has moved into the position held by the Western genre for most of the 20th century, when it served as a useful metaphorical way of discussing immigration, Americanization, urbanization, American identity, changing conceptions of race and gender, individualism, capitalism, modernism, and so many other central cultural concerns. In the Cold War, the Western became crucial to America's image of itself. Think of the Cold War as a Western—two diametrically opposed cultures in a twilight struggle that could end in an apocalypse. In Westerns, Indians (using the language of Westerns) often threaten the wholesale destruction of the settlers, and the stories often end in an apocalyptic, fiery extirpation of Indian towns and an expulsion of Indians from the settled territory. During the Cold War, especially at its height in the 1950s, Westerns dominated television and were consistently popular at the movies. This popularity can be traced to many factors, but at some level the genre's metaphors worked well to express social tensions. According to Thomas Schatz, genres are privileged story forms in which social tensions are brought to life in narratives and ritualistically resolved. Popular genres are those that can best animate and resolve social tensions through their metaphors.[1]

In fact, like Westerns, superhero stories depict an "epic moment" when civilization is threatened but the forces of savagery—whether represented as Indians or outlaws in Westerns or villains in superhero stories—are defeated. Whereas the violence in Westerns was in the service of containment (trying to keep the "Reds" on the reservation, as with the Truman Doctrine and the West's attempt to limit communist expansion), the violence in superhero stories arises as a last resort (as with the Powell Doctrine after the Cold War), engaged in by the superhero because of the implacable threat posed by the supervillain, which ordinary authorities are unable to combat effectively.

Emblematic of this cultural shift in storied metaphor from Western to superhero is the choice of adjective to describe some modern presidents. If Ronald Reagan was the first modern "cowboy" president of the United States (and George W. Bush the second one), Barack Obama is its first "superhero" president. He was frequently portrayed as a superhero in editorial cartoons and websites, and at the 63rd Annual Alfred E. Smith Memorial Foundation Dinner in 2008, a charity roast organized by the Catholic Archdiocese of New York for the benefit of needy children, Obama played off the image of himself as a savior, saying, "Contrary to the rumors you have heard, I was not born in a manger. I was actually born on Krypton and sent here by my father, Jor-El, to save the planet Earth."

The current popularity of superhero movies seems to demonstrate the hold the genre has on the public, and these movies take up current real-world issues. Iron Man, in his first movie, directly takes on fanatical terrorists in Afghanistan. In *The Dark Knight*, the Joker explicitly uses terror and nihilistic aggression to forward his ends, and Batman employs both warrantless surveillance and extraordinary rendition to battle him. In *Spider-Man 2*, when Doctor Octopus moves to finish off the Amazing Arachnid on an elevated train in New York, the passengers step forward to defend the unconscious and unmasked Spider-Man in a scene reminiscent of the real-life heroic actions of United 93 passengers who stood up to the hijackers.

And the superhero is a figure that touches centrally on the likely future of humans. Baseball player Alexander Rodriguez explained his steroid use as a response to the pressure he felt to perform at a superhuman level (because of the chemical enhancements employed by other players).[2] A-Rod's fear of losing to "superhumans" recurs in superhero comics. For instance, Lex Luthor hates Superman because he sees the Kryptonian as marking an end to human potential and achievements, the end of human dreams: "All of us—everyone—deserves a chance at greatness. All that takes is the belief that it exists. But his existence threatens not just that belief, but our existence. I believe there's something inherently dangerous when something real becomes mythic. I believe when that happens we lose the part of ourselves that yearns to be great. Because when faced with a myth? We can't win."[3]

This same concern surfaces in the graphic novels *Kingdom Come*, *Watchmen*, and *Miracleman*, in the X-Men, and in countless other superhero comics, as well as in films like *Gattaca*. Widespread steroid use means that players who don't use can't compete. Barry Bonds became a myth when he broke Hank Aaron's home run record— and it appears that no merely human player, unaided by superpowers, may be able to break Bond's record, driving home Luthor's point. That mythic future of superbeings among mere humans is becoming a reality through the GRIN technologies (genetics, robotics, information, and nanotechnology) that promise to transform us—or perhaps just those of us who can afford them—into superhumans. Those who can't transform might be left behind. Superheroes and their stories allow us to explore these possible futures; exploring what the superhero is aids our understanding of our recent past, contemporary political and social situation, and future. That's why the question "What is a superhero?" matters.

So how is this question to be answered, and whose answers count? We approached this problem from a shared history of bringing scholars and comics professionals together to discuss comics and superheroes. Peter co-founded and co-chairs the Comics Arts Conference (CAC), an academic conference held during the San Diego Comic-Con International. The CAC operates to bring scholars and comics professionals together in dialogue with the public via the medium of the academic conference at a comic book convention in order to break down the walls between the academy and the industry and to share the insights of both with the public; it's an effort at public intellectualism. The professionals bring their real-world, concrete experience of struggling with the demands of crafting a story, editorial directives, sales, and appealing to audiences. Scholars can step back from the daily grind and pecuniary concerns of publishing to look at the big picture and investigate superheroes across a range of contexts through their scholarly training and methodological tools. Bringing scholars and professionals together brings theory and practice together and shines a dual light that illuminates the topic from multiple perspectives. Peter and Robin met through a CAC panel that Robin organized in 2009, "Is the Joker a Psychopath? You Decide!" that perfectly illustrated the value of bringing scholars and professionals together, and she and Peter were joined by psychology professor Travis Langley, Joker creator Jerry Robinson, Adam West of TV's *Batman*, famed "Joker-fish" writer Steve Englehart, and *Batman* film producer Michael Uslan. Robin and Travis Langley explained the psychology of psychopathy, and the superhero professionals on the panel discussed how the depiction of the Joker across media enacted the traits associated with psychopaths. Either side of this equation on its own would have left out what the other offered. Like this Joker panel, *What Is a Superhero?* brings scholars and professionals into dialogue through the discussion of this central question.

Essentially, creators encode their ideas of what constitutes a superhero through their depictions of the characters, and scholars decode what constitutes a superhero through their academic analyses of rendered depictions. We wanted to represent both ends of that equation to get at how the definition of the superhero is engaged when creators create and how it is understood and explained—how meaning is made and made usable. Space constraints forced us to invite only a fraction of the people whose views we wanted to hear. On the creator side, for this volume we restricted ourselves to comic book writers and editors, as it is a story's words that carry the bulk of the message and morals. We made sure to invite creators who represent various generations of comic book stories from the Golden Age to today, who have introduced major characters or revisions of characters, and who worked on superhero movies and television shows.

For scholars, we wanted a spread of disciplines. Too often in the past, comics studies has been biased toward scholars of literature for reasons grounded in the political economy of academia and the fact that literary scholars are inherently comfortable working with narrative texts. The scholars we recruited as contributors come from a range of disciplines—philosophy, literary history and criticism, cultural studies, religious studies, art and visual aesthetics, psychology, and women's studies—and employ a wide mix of theoretical lenses, including phenomenology, genre criticism, literary analysis, feminist theory, deconstruction, communications theory, media theory, and popular culture theory. Academic disciplines construct different ways of understanding reality and establishing truth and employ different theories and methodologies—lenses that shape the way objects of inquiry are interpreted. Each discipline tends to have its own way, or ways, of seeing that determine what counts as evidence, what sorts of objects are looked at, and how the interpretation is presented.

It is our hope that by bringing together creators from across comics history and media and scholars from across the university, we have cooked up a tasty stew of answers, ultimately leaving it in your hands to decide what a superhero is.

What is the superhero? We can't answer that question in the Introduction, but we have arranged the book around certain foci that should provide for comparative reading. First, in every essay there is a direct statement of the author's answer to the title question. As you read, look for the phrase "a superhero is." Our intention is that you might pull these answers out and compare them—which ones lean toward the general or universal answer? Which toward culturally and historically specific answers? Which answers delineate specific conditions or criteria or limit who gets admitted to the superhero clubhouse, and which answers are more expansive and inclusive?

Is there an answer to the question, "What is a superhero?" Maybe; maybe not. But here are 25 attempts to provide one by people who have built careers making and studying the superhero. Enjoy.

NOTES

1. Thomas Schatz. (1981). *Hollywood Genres: Formulas, Filmmaking, and the Studio System.* New York: McGraw Hill, pp. 29–31.

2. Peter Gammons, "Rodriguez: 'Sorry and deeply regretful.' " February 9, 2009, http://sports. espn.go.com/mlb/news/story?id=3895281

3. Brian Azzarello and Lee Bermejo. (2005). *Lex Luthor: Man of Steel.* New York: DC Comics, Chapter 3.

What Is a Superhero?

Super and Hero:
Powers and Mission

What defines a superhero? The word itself gives us a couple of clues. The super part indicates powers or abilities that are significantly greater than those of the average person (though they need not be "beyond those of mortal men" or women). The hero part indicates that the gifted individual acts heroically—not just on a handful of occasions, but repeatedly. The superhero consistently tries to do the right thing. He or she has a mission. The essays in this section explore the role of those powers and missions and how they help to define superheroes and create the genre itself.

ONE

The Hero Defines the Genre, the Genre Defines the Hero

Peter Coogan

Peter Coogan is director of the Institute for Comics Studies, co-founder and co-chair of the Comics Arts Conference, and an instructor at Washington University in St. Louis, MO. He holds a Ph.D. in American Studies and authored *Superhero: The Secret Origin of the Superhero*, a monograph on the development, history, and functioning of the superhero genre. He is a nationally known commentator on comics and superheroes, has a semi-regular pundit gig on the *Major Spoilers Podcast*, and is co-editor of this volume.

The superhero is the protagonist of the superhero genre. The first superhero— the founding character in the superhero genre—was Superman, whose debut in *Action Comics* #1 (cover date June 1938) established the major conventions of the superhero genre. What made Superman different from the heroes of the science fiction, fantasy, pulp, Western, war, and jungle adventure genres? It was the specific conventions—*mission*, *powers*, and *identity*—that coalesced in Superman's heroic portrayal, and which were then imitated and repeated by other comic book creators. Imitation and repetition are important—without them, a genre doesn't exist. Every genre has a central dynamic: Westerns are about civilization triumphing over savagery, detective stories detail the solution of a mystery, and superhero stories concern the responsible use of extraordinary power in the service of justice. The definition of the superhero, as the protagonist of the superhero genre, written dictionary style, is

> **Su•per•he•ro** (soo'per hîr'o) *n.*, *pl.* -roes. A heroic character with a universal, selfless, prosocial mission; who possesses superpowers—extraordinary abilities, advanced technology, or highly developed physical and/or mental skills (including mystical abilities); who has a superhero identity embodied in a code name and iconic costume, which typically express his biography or character, powers, and origin (transformation from ordinary person to superhero); and is generically distinct, i.e. can be distinguished from characters of related genres (fantasy, science fiction, detective, etc.) by a preponderance of generic conventions. Often superheroes have dual identities, the ordinary one of which is usually a closely guarded secret. —**superheroic**, *adj*. Also **super hero, super-hero.**[1]

This dictionary definition is concise and specific to the superhero genre.[*]

---

[*] This definition is also applicable. In this volume, Richard Reynolds and John Jennings employ this definition as part of their discussions.

The superhero's *mission* is to fight evil and protect the innocent; this fight is universal, prosocial, and selfless. The superhero's mission must fit in with the existing, professed mores of society, and it must not be intended to benefit or further the superhero. The mission fulfills the *hero* part of superhero. We see the concept of the superhero's mission operating when the news media in our world designate people as "local superheroes," ordinary citizens who selflessly act to better their community. It's the selflessness and the prosocial nature of their acts that cause such people to be labeled as superheroes, a metaphor that is rooted in the superhero genre. When George W. Bush and Ronald Reagan were called "cowboys," both the speakers and the audiences recognized the metaphorical application of the term *cowboy*. No one would mean to imply, nor would anyone infer, that either of these presidents was a ranch hand who drove cattle. *Cowboy* here is a metaphor rooted in the Western genre, not in the actual lives of 19th century employees of cattle barons. The metaphoric use of *superhero* is similarly rooted in the superhero genre and in the protagonists' selfless, prosocial mission.

The mission convention is essential to the superhero genre because someone who does not act selflessly to aid others in times of need is not heroic and therefore not a hero. But the prosocial mission is not unique to the genre. Superman's mission is to be a "champion of the oppressed...sworn to devote his existence to helping those in need"—that is, to "benefit mankind."[2] This mission is not essentially different from that of the pulp adventurer Doc Savage, whose "purpose was to go here and there, from one end of the world to another, looking for excitement and adventure, striving to help those who needed help, punishing those who deserved it."[3] Nor does Superman's mission differ materially from the missions of the dime novel or pulp and radio heroes of the late 19th and early 20th centuries.

The superhero's mission does, however, distinguish him or her from certain other hero types. Many Western and science fiction heroes do not have the universal mission of the superhero or pulp vigilante because they are not seeking to "do good" for the sake of doing good.* Instead, many of these heroes reluctantly get drawn into defending a community. In contrast, superheroes actively seek to protect their communities by preventing harm to all individuals and to right wrongs committed by criminals and other villains.

Powers—or superpowers, to emphasize the exaggeration inherent in the superhero genre—are often put forward as the central, defining element of the superhero; they put the *super* in superhero. They are all those abilities and qualities that raise a person's performance above that of ordinary people. Often these are thought of as supernatural abilities—abilities that defy the laws of physics in some way—which is why people often claim that Batman does not have superpowers. But superpowers need not violate

---

* Pulp vigilantes of the 1930s and 1940s, such as The Shadow, the Spider, the Phantom Detective, or the Avenger, fought crime much like superheroes, though usually with a more investigative bent. Most had physical abilities that stretched plausibility, but in general they did not have superpowers that defied the laws of physics. They used code names and disguises, but not costumes that iconically expressed their identities. On the whole, they killed their enemies freely and easily, even gleefully, without the restraint typically shown by superheroes.

the laws of physics. Wildcat and the Golden Age Atom are merely highly trained athletes, but their physical abilities allow them to interact with the godlike Spectre or Dr. Fate as part of the superhero community.* Nor do superpowers need to be inherent in the body of the superhero. Although Tony Stark's genius may have enabled him to create his advanced armor for Iron Man, his genius is not a superpower; rather, it is the armor that provides Iron Man's superpowers. The same is true of Hal Jordan's willpower: It makes him an excellent wielder of the power of the Green Lantern ring, but it is the ring and not the willpower that gives him his superpowers. Superpowers can come from extraordinary abilities, like the X-Men's mutant abilities (*extra-ordinary* in the literal sense); advanced technology, like Iron Man's armor; or highly developed physical or mental skills, like Batman's martial arts prowess or his supreme tactical abilities. Superpowers can also include mystical abilities that result from years of study and training, like Dr. Strange's mastery of the mystic arts.†

Superpowers distinguish Superman from his pulp and science fiction predecessors and contemporaries. Each of Superman's powers amplifies the abilities of the science fiction supermen who came before him. Hugo Danner, the protagonist of Philip Wylie's novel of social commentary, *Gladiator* (1930), was bulletproof, super-strong, and super-fast.‡ In the first issue of *Action Comics*, published in 1938, Superman displays super-strength, super-speed, super-leaping, and invulnerability at only slightly greater levels than Danner. Over time, though, Superman's powers went far beyond merely exaggerating the strength, speed, and toughness of ordinary human beings as science fiction supermen's powers had done; he gained the powers of flight, heat and x-ray vision, super-cooling breath, faster-than-light speed, and even time travel. Superman also differed from science fiction supermen in that he used his extraordinary

* Wildcat is secretly heavyweight boxing champion Ted Grant, who dresses in a black cat costume to fight crime and has no paranormal superpowers, only his boxing expertise; he debuted in *Sensation Comics* #1 (January 1942). The Golden Age Atom is diminutive college student Al Pratt, a 5'1" weakling who trained in boxing and bodybuilding to overcome his poor childhood health; he first appeared in *All-American Comics* #19 (October 1940). The Spectre is a nearly omnipotent spirit of vengeance who takes the form of deceased police officer Jim Corrigan to grimly punish evildoers; the Spectre's first story appeared in *More Fun Comics* #52 (February1940), and he was created by Superman writer Jerry Siegel. The mystical Dr. Fate is actually Kent Nelson, son of an archeologist who died while opening the tomb of the ancient wizard Nabu. Nabu trained the orphaned boy in powerful magic. Dr. Fate first appeared in *More Fun Comics* #55 (May 1940). All four are DC Comics characters.

† Dr. Strange is Dr. Stephen Strange, an arrogant neurosurgeon who is injured in a car accident and seeks healing under the tutelage of the Ancient One in the Himalayas, who trains him to be the Master of the Mystic Arts. He is a Marvel Comics character and debuted in 1963.

‡ Hugo Danner's father gives him in utero injections that give Hugo enhanced strength, speed, and invulnerability, but his life ends in futility because he cannot find a place in society to employ his superior abilities. *Gladiator* was part of Wylie's commentary on the plight of the superior man in a society that he felt prized mediocrity. Jerry Siegel likely took inspiration from *Gladiator* for Superman, though this supposition has never been definitely confirmed or disproven.

powers within contemporary society in pursuit of his selfless prosocial mission. Prior to Superman, these sorts of powers were typically employed in narratives set far in the past or future or on other planets, not in a realistic version of modern, urban America.

The *identity* convention is the clearest marker of the superhero genre. The identity is composed of two elements: the *code name* (e.g., "Superman" and "Spider-Man"), with the secret identity being a customary counterpart to the code name (e.g., "Clark Kent" and "Peter Parker"), and the *costume*. The code name conveys some aspect of the character, typically his or her mission or powers or the character's origin or personality. "Superman" indicates someone who is a superior person, the peak of physical, mental, and moral evolution. "Captain America" indicates someone whose patriotic mission is paramount. "Spider-Man" indicates spider powers. "Batman" refers to the bat that flew through Bruce Wayne's window and symbolizes the fear he inspires that turns him into a mythic figure of terror for the criminal underground of Gotham. "The Hulk" conveys, as Stan Lee learned from a thesaurus, "a gargantuan creature, a being of awesome strength coupled with a dull and sluggish thinking process."[4] Superman's code name is particularly important, as it is likely the source of *superhero* as a designation for the characters that sprung from his popularity.

Like the code name, the costume also conveys a sense of the superhero's mission, powers, origin, or personality. For instance, Superman's costume is made from blankets that accompanied him from Krypton in the rocket ship, and the *S* chevron on his chest is his El family crest; the costume represents his Kryptonian heritage and the source of his powers. Captain America's costume is a stylized American flag. Spider-Man's spider chevron announces his powers, and Batman's bat chevron records the bat that inspired his identity.

Similar to his code name, Superman's costume formed the template for superhero costumes—form-fitting tights with shorts worn over them, a cape, a chevron, a belt, and boots; these are the basic components of a costume. Batman added the cowl and mask, and Captain America (among others) ditched the cape. But Superman's costume remains the base from which other superhero's outfits are built.

Further, the costume announces the superhero and places him or her within the superhero community. In *Nightwing* #102, Dick Grayson, who had recently quit being Robin, visits Superman in Metropolis to get some guidance from the Man of Steel about what to do with his life. During the trip, Grayson and Superman separately face down members of a political hit squad. The assassin facing Superman knows exactly what the Man of Steel is there to do—stop him. But when Dick Grayson, wearing jeans and a windbreaker with a bandana over his face, drops down on the ledge where the assassin is perched, the villain wonders who he is and why he's there. Grayson thinks, "Without the mask and colors I had to explain myself."[5] The costume explains why the hero is fighting crime; without the costume, Dick Grayson has no immediately understandable purpose on that ledge—there's no community or context to which he belongs.

The costume continues to announce the superhero genre to this day. Put a kid in a bathing suit with goggles and flippers, and he's ready for the beach. Tie part of a towel around his neck so the rest flows down his back, and suddenly he's Beach Boy!

The cape alone—in this case, a towel doing double-duty—stands for the idea of the superhero. Superheroes are often referred to as "capes" or "masks" by the fictional cops and criminals who populate superhero stories. In fact, the superhero can be suggested without depicting the costume directly. A man using both hands to open his shirt to reveal his chest, bare or clothed, is so suggestive of superheroes—specifically Superman—that DC Comics has trademarked the pose and threatened legal action to protect it.*

These three elements—mission, powers, and identity—establish the core of the genre. But specific superheroes can exist who do not fully demonstrate all three of these elements. This apparent indeterminacy originates in the nature of genre. No one example within a genre displays every convention of its genre, but all examples from a genre share common elements that form a "complicated network of similarities overlapping and crisscrossing: sometimes overall similarities, sometimes similarities of detail" that can be best thought of as "family resemblances."[6] These family resemblances are all the conventions that mark a character as belonging to the superhero genre, and which I designate as generic distinction.† Examples of superheroes without all three core elements of mission, powers, and identity abound. The Hulk is a superhero without a mission: At times he seems absolutely antisocial, and his adventures do not typically arise from his attempts to fight crime or improve the world. Batman was originally designed as a superhero without superpowers.[7] Wildcat and the Atom are highly trained athletic fighters and lack even Batman's advanced technology (which Batman lacked in his early appearances). The Fantastic Four debuted without costumes (although they did have code names). But whichever primary convention is weak in these heroes, they fully possess the other two, and their stories are full of the other conventions of the superhero genre—costumed supervillains, science fiction technology, superhero teams, headquarters, supporting casts, and all the other accoutrements of superherodom. The preponderance of conventions, or generic distinction, determines the identification of a character as a superhero (as the protagonist of the superhero genre) if one or more elements of the core triad are weak or missing.

This sort of superhero—the one with mission, powers, and identity—is the genre *superhero* and is distinct from heroes of other genres who are sometimes called superheroes. Such characters—Buffy the Vampire Slayer, The Shadow, Beowulf, Luke Skywalker—all do good while using their superior physical or mental skills; they are heroes who are super, or super heroes.‡ Generic distinction—the preponderance or totality of generic conventions—roots these characters firmly in other genres

---

* I have had personal conversations with DC representatives who have confirmed this claim and with an artist who was threatened with legal action over the use of this image.

† Kurt Busiek, in his essay for this volume, uses the term "superhero milieu" to identify the conventions that combine to form generic distinction.

‡ The space between words that distinguishes a superhero from a super hero is like the one that distinguishes the adjective *everyday* (meaning ordinary) from the phrase *every day* (meaning daily). Although *everyday* and *every day* get mixed up in usage, they mean different things. The same is true of *superhero* (a superhero genre protagonist) and *super hero* (a hero who is super).

(respectively, horror, pulp vigilante, epic, and science fiction), which means that while (as Meatloaf put it) "two out of three ain't bad," it's not enough.[8] There is a distinction between these heroes who are super and superheroes. In fact, this distinction is widely and intuitively, if not formally, understood. Writers who include Zorro, Buffy the Vampire Slayer, Jack Bauer, or John McClane (Bruce Willis's character from the *Die Hard* series) still distinguish between these heroes who are super and genre superheroes. The distinction is indicated through phrases like "the super-powered, costumed, comic book variety," "a costumed superhero," or "the comic book crowd"[9] because the difference between genre superheroes like Superman, Batman, Captain America, and Spider-Man and heroes who are super is well understood, if sometimes difficult to articulate. This difficulty is rooted in the slipperiness of genre generally and the indistinct boundaries between genres due to the sharing of conventions across genres, and it arises primarily when someone attempts to define the superhero. If *Zorro 3* and *Iron Man 3* were to come out the same weekend and a friend said, "Let's go see a superhero movie," your friend would mean *Iron Man*. But ask that friend to define "superhero," and in comes Zorro. The distinction between Iron Man as a superhero and Zorro as a costumed vigilante is understood, but the act of articulating the definition causes this distinction to dissolve.

The reason for the general indeterminacy of the definition of the superhero lies in the way the genre is understood. The superhero genre is a genre of its own, but most people don't recognize it in the way they do science fiction, or Westerns, or fantasy. These other genres, like all genres, have their own definitional difficulties, but the difficulties with the superhero genre are particularly knotty because the superhero genre shares its primary conventions of mission, powers, and identity, as well as secondary conventions such as supervillains, advanced technology, urban settings, and helpful authority figures, with many other genres, particularly adventure genres. Adventure genres—which include superhero, war, Western, and fantasy—feature a "central fantasy" of the hero "overcoming obstacles and dangers and accomplishing some important and moral mission."[10] Luke Skywalker puts himself in harm's way to defeat Darth Vader and the Empire, as does Flash Gordon in his struggle against Ming the Merciless, as does James Bond when he takes down Goldfinger or Dr. No. These heroes clearly have selfless, prosocial missions, so distinguishing between them and superheroes is understandably difficult. The superhero mission's universality is one thing that differentiates it from the missions of these other heroes. Luke Skywalker doesn't go out on patrol to stop muggers on Tatooine. Flash Gordon largely limits his activities to Mongo. James Bond serves M16; he doesn't diffuse hostage crises or respond to burglar alarms.

Powers are common to heroic characters in many adventure genres, whether genuinely supernatural powers of mythological heroes such as the strength of Hercules, the heightened human powers of legendary heroes such as the endurance of Roland, or the abilities of heroes from genres more rooted in a realistic depiction of the laws of physics, such as the ability of *24*'s Jack Bauer to withstand torture or the fighting abilities of *Die Hard*'s John McClane. Jack Bauer's and John McClane's abilities certainly seem beyond those of ordinary people, even if they are not at the level of Hercules' strength, Beowulf's grip, or Luke Skywalker's Jedi mind tricks. Although the powers of Superman, Green

Lantern, Dr. Strange, and the Spectre do seem to be exaggerated or expand beyond the limits of those of most other genre heroes, these superheroes' powers are different in degree rather than in kind relative to the powers of heroes of other genres. Moreover, many "street-level" superheroes like Batman, Daredevil, or Wildcat operate at power levels far below those of science fiction heroes such as Neo of the *Matrix* trilogy or fantasy heroes like Harry Potter, so superpowers are not distinct to the superhero genre.

Both the code name and costume portions of the identity convention are shared with other genres, but much less frequently than mission and powers. Pulp vigilantes like The Shadow, the Spider, the Phantom Detective, the Crimson Clown, the Green Hornet, and the Black Bat employ code names in the same way superheroes do. But outside the pulp vigilante genre, code names are rarer and operate in different ways. Although Buffy is known as "the Slayer," the Slayer is not a public identity in the way the identities of the Fantastic Four or Spider-Man are. Residents of Sunnydale are not aware of the Slayer the way the residents of Marvel's New York are of Mr. Fantastic and the Invisible Woman. The Fantastic Four's code names operate similarly to stage names like Madonna, Lady Gaga, or Ke$ha—these are public names that everyone recognizes. Just as some fans know the names Madonna Ciccone, Stefani Germanotta, or Kesha Sebert, some residents of Marvel's New York know the names Reed Richards and Susan Storm. "The Slayer" does not keep Buffy's family and friends safe from harm the way "Spider-Man" does Peter Parker's Aunt May. Nor does "the Slayer" entail a different personality, as the Superman identity does for Clark Kent. In the television series *Dark Angel*, the protagonist Max Guevera is never called "Dark Angel" in a story; the name is completely external to the world of the story and is known only to viewers. So the parallels between the superhero genre's use of the code name convention and similar uses in other genres are much more limited.

The costume, while not absolutely unique to the superhero genre, is identified much more with the superhero genre than with other genres. Genre superheroes are often referred to as costumed superheroes or long-underwear heroes (as well as "capes" and "masks"). The producers of *Smallville* wanted to hold off on identifying the show with the larger Superman mythos and the superhero genre, so they employed the motto "no flights, no tights" when thinking about the show (highlighting two main identifying features of Superman—and hence superhero—stories).[11] More importantly, a superhero's costume tends to be a visual embodiment of the character's mission, powers, origin, or personality in a way that pulp vigilante costumes are not, and it also tends to be much more iconic in terms of how the costume expresses the connection with the mission, powers, origin, or personality. Zorro is often put forward as a costume wearer, but his all-black outfit, cape, mask, and broad-brimmed hat do not iconically suggest "fox," which is what *zorro* means in Spanish. The Shadow's black cloak enables him to hide in the shadows, but it does not suggest the idea of a shadow in the way that Iron Man's armor suggests a man made of iron. Even the costume of the Black Bat, a pulp vigilante who wears an all-black body suit with a scalloped cape that suggests bat wings, is not as iconic as Batman's pointy-eared cowl and bat chevron. The chevron—the chest shield or logo that has been central to the superhero genre since the debut of Superman in 1938—is a convention of the costume that is almost unique to the superhero genre, and it is probably the clearest marker of the genre.

The superhero genre shares many of its other conventions—the supervillain, the helpful authority figure, the sanctum sanctorum, the team, the sidekick, and even the dual identity—with other genres but usually has emphases that are specific to it in the way these conventions are deployed or have come to be firmly identified with the superhero genre. The damsel in distress, who is often the hero's love interest, is common to adventure genres in general. But the two-person love triangle—best embodied by the Superman–Lois Clark relationship in which the woman is attracted to the superhero who spurns her advances, while she similarly spurns the advances of the secret-identity alter ego who pursues her—is firmly identified with the superhero genre.

The superhero genre has changed over time because, like all genres, it responds to changes in the culture. But the core conventions of mission, powers, and identity have remained stable. These primary conventions are an economical way to indicate firmly that a heroic character is a superhero. So what is a superhero? A superhero is the protagonist of the superhero genre. Other heroic figures—whether real or fictional— are called superheroes because they are super (they have powers) and/or heroes (with selfless, prosocial missions). But these uses of *superhero* can be considered metaphoric references to the superhero genre. All answers to the question "What is a superhero?" are ultimately rooted in the superhero genre.

NOTES

1. Peter Coogan, *Superhero: The Secret Origin of a Genre* (MonkeyBrain Books, 2006), p. 30. I have added "universal" to the description of the mission to clarify an aspect of the superhero mission that distinguishes it from those of other genres.
2. Jerry Siegel and Joe Shuster, *Action Comics* #1, June 1938, p. 1.
3. Kenneth Robeson [Lester Dent], *Man of Bronze*. New York: Bantam, 1933/1964, p. 4. Doc Savage is Clark Savage, Jr., a pulp adventurer whose adventures were published by Street and Smith from 1933 to 1949 and has appeared in numerous paperback and comic book revivals, as well as a campy 1975 feature film, *Doc Savage: The Man of Bronze*, starring Ron Ely.
4. Stan Lee, *Origins of Marvel Comics*. New York: Simon and Schuster, 1974, p. 75.
5. Scott Beatty, Chuck Dixon, and Scott McDaniel, "Bombs Away!" *Nightwing* 102 (March 2005), p. 8.
6. Ludwig Wittgenstein, cited in Brian Henderson, "Romantic Comedy Today: Semi-Tough or Impossible?" *Film Genre Reader*. Ed. Barry Keith Grant. Austin, TX: U. of Texas P., 1986, p. 314.
7. Bob Kane and Tom Andrae, *Batman and Me*. Forrestville, CA: Eclipse Books, 1989, p. 99.
8. Jim Steinman, "Two Out of Three Ain't Bad," on Meatloaf, *Bat Out of Hell*, Epic Records, 1977.
9. Joe Quesada, "the super-powered, costumed, comic book variety"; Jennifer Stuller, "a costumed superhero"; and Kurt Busiek, "the comic book crowd."
10. John Cawelti, *Adventure, Mystery, and Romance: Formula Stories as Art and Popular Culture*. Chicago: University of Chicago Press, 1976, p. 40.
11. Christine Mersch, "Alfred Gough." *Writers Digest*, February 11, 2008. www.writersdigest. com/article/Alfred_Gough

TWO

We Could Be Heroes

Will Brooker

Will Brooker is Professor in Film and Cultural Studies at Kingston University, London. His Ph.D. thesis focused on a cultural history of Batman and involved a three-year study of the Dark Knight across all media from 1939 to 1999. The research was published as *Batman Unmasked* and earned him the title Dr. Batman in the media. He has since published widely on popular culture and its audiences.

Superheroes are about wish fulfillment. They're about imagining a better world and creating an alternate version of yourself—bigger, brighter, bolder than the real thing—to patrol and protect it. That's the way it's always been, right from the start. That's how it was for Jerry Siegel and Joe Shuster, misfit young men from immigrant families who dreamed up a Superman in the 1930s; that's how it was for Bob Kahn, a little later, sketching a Bat-Man who could soar above the roofs of his run-down Bronx neighborhood. Kahn even changed his own name, hiding his Jewish roots in a new brand—Bob Kane—and a carefully crafted logo; when he put his signature to Bat-Man, he also confirmed a new identity for himself, and he made sure it rhymed with Bruce Wayne.

The best heroes are those with hidden hurt and secret wounds—the ones who channel some of their creators' outsider status and reflect back some of their readers' insecurity. Superman is arguably the least interesting of the bunch. He's annoyingly untraumatized for someone who witnessed the destruction of his home planet and grew up as an alien on Earth, and his stuttering, stumbling alter-ego persona Clark Kent is just a front. Most of his pals in the first wave of superhero comics were similarly confident heroes, in the mold of cinema's handsome matinee idols—sure, they had a token weakness, like Superman's Kryptonite or the Green Lantern's vulnerability to wood,* and they suffered the odd romantic quarrel with their girlfriends, but at heart they were square-jawed, barrel-chested, all-American, stand-up guys. Even Wonder Woman, an Amazon from the peacefully feminist Paradise Island with presumably no stake in World War II, integrated herself happily into "Man's World," dated a U.S. Army officer, and fought the Nazis. Batman's sidekick, Robin, was meant to provide a way in for the young reader, but again, he was pretty perky for an orphan.

Marvel Comics did something new in the 1960s by introducing a superhero with a genuinely geeky private life. Teen boys could see themselves for the first time in Peter Parker, the bullied bookworm, whose life was much closer to theirs than Clark Kent's metropolitan whirl or Robin's high-wire history as a circus acrobat. When Parker transformed into Spider-Man, his becoming a *man* was as significant as his getting

---

* Editors' note: The ring of the original Green Lantern from the Golden Age was ineffective against wood. In the Silver Age, this limitation was changed to the color yellow.

the abilities of a spider, and Spidey's confident wise-cracking was as important as the web-slinging and wall-crawling. Sam Raimi's *Spider-Man* film of 2002 had the right idea, depicting Parker's transition through sequences of sticky web fluid and embarrassing homemade costumes—becoming a man can be a messy business.

Superhero mythology is about escape, about creating an alternative identity and becoming someone different, someone better. Arguably, superheroes are at their finest when they're the alter-ego creations of geeks and loners, not handsome hunks. In Grant Morrison's *Doom Patrol* comic of the early 1990s, it's clear that the author understood that: it's a story of misfits and rejects, including puny Wally Sage, who sketched a muscle-bound hero called Flex Mentallo and brought his imaginary friend to life. Together, Wally and Flex look like the "before" and "after" pictures in the Charles Atlas ads: the boy who got sand kicked in his face, and the superman he wants to become. "There is a better world," runs a caption in *Doom Patrol*, quoting Morrissey, a singer who fully understands the lost and the lonely; "Well...there must be."

Perhaps the most poignant example of the way a misfit can transform himself through a mask is Rorschach, from Alan Moore's epic graphic novel *Watchmen*. Rorschach first appears as a stone-cold, hard-boiled urban vigilante dressed in a private eye trench coat. His face is obscured by shifting patterns of black and white, symbolizing his binary worldview: "Never compromise. Even in the face of Armageddon." One of the story's major twists is the revelation that Rorschach is Walter Kovacs, a bigoted loner who wears platform shoes, lives in a tiny room, never washes his stinking trench coat, and slurps beans straight from the can. But along with the squalor, the sadness, and the madness of Kovacs's existence, we're shown how he turned out that way—a childhood of beatings, bullying, and abuse—and we understand why he needed a new identity: to escape his own real life. His mask isn't just a mask. The mask is his face, a face he can bear to look at in the mirror. How many teenagers, male and female, have felt ugly and unlovable and wished they could cover their face with a clean, anonymous blank? Rorschach's transformation is far more important than just putting on a cloak and thinking of a cool name. It's the only way he can live with himself. Becoming a superhero—or an anti-hero, in his case—is a new start, a new history. That's one reason that an origin story, the tale of how a character gained his or her identity and chose his or her costume, is invariably of a "secret origin": The stories bury the old, battered, weaker self and give the character a new life as someone braver and bolder.

Batman, of course, is the prime example of the self-made superhero. His appeal lies primarily in the fact that he's a human being. He's trained to the point of mental and physical perfection, but his powers are all based in human ingenuity and determination. Any reader could become Batman. Sure, you'd have to suffer a childhood trauma, inherit a fortune, hone your body, study forensics, and craft your own gadgets, but if you really put your mind to it, you could become Batman—or that's what generations of fans have told themselves.* Christian Bale's recent casting in *The Dark Knight*

---

* Editors' note: Author E. Paul Zehr argues in *Becoming Batman: The Possibility of a Superhero* (Baltimore: Johns Hopkins Press, 2009) that it would be physically possible to achieve Batman's level of performance, particularly for a crime-fighting career of only two years.

Trilogy (2005–2012) only confirms the theory: Bale, according to director Christopher Nolan, bulked up, built muscle, learned martial arts, and climbed to the pinnacles of sky-scrapers to inhabit the role.

Christopher Nolan's Batman films are distinctive because of their realism; they ditch the camp and the gothic fantasy of earlier incarnations and reimagine the gadgets and costumes in plausibly militaristic terms—Batarangs become throwing knives, the Batsuit becomes spray-painted Kevlar armor, and the Batmobile becomes a tank. Similarly, *Watchmen*'s big idea was to depict superheroes realistically, imagining how they'd work in a world very much like our own; thus, a vigilante like Rorschach is revealed as an unhy-gienic conspiracy nut. But of course, our real world is severely lacking in costumed heroes. Though we've read about their adventures for over 70 years in the comics, nobody has ever made a living out of dressing up and fighting crime. It would be unreasonable to expect a godlike patriot like Superman or the science fiction powers of Green Lantern, but we've never even had more plausible hard-ass masked vigilantes like Rorschach or self-made city guardians like Batman. Maybe that's because the concept of a masked protector just outside the boundaries of the law doesn't comfortably cross over. When real-life vigilantes do hit the headlines, they're not cool and stylish, but dangerous, pathetic nutjobs with a gun and a grudge. When guys dress up in superhero costumes to protest a cause or raise awareness, they invariably look saggy and paunchy rather than sleek and dynamic.*

So, is ours a world without superheroes? Not entirely. Our versions do dress up, they just don't fight crime. In our own alternate universe, the closest we get to larger-than-life costumed characters are entertainers rather than vigilantes—ordinary people who trans-form themselves into bigger, brighter versions of themselves, and in doing so offer the same promise of escape and empowerment to their followers.

Media icons with secret identities have been around at least as long as the comic book heroes. In the 1900s, Florence Lawrence, the first-ever movie star, was branded "The Biograph Girl" as if she were a real-life superheroine, and just as characters like Batman have passed on their cape, cowl, and code name to others, Florence shared her new name with another girl, Mary Pickford. In the 1930s and 1940s, when Superman and his co-stars made their first appearances in comics, Archibald Leach and Marion Morrison were ditching their slightly wimpy names and recreating themselves as the debonair Cary Grant and the solidly masculine John Wayne; a little later, a model-actress called Norma Jeane Mortenson followed suit. Her chosen identity, Marilyn Monroe, even sounds like a superhero name—or a superhero's secret alter ego, along the lines of Peter Parker and Reed Richards—and perhaps more tellingly, the double "M," which she felt was a lucky omen, looks like a superhero logo, a lightning bolt or zigzag.†

In the 1950s, when Elvis took on the brand "The King,"‡ British singers with everyday names dreamed up flashier, manlier, comic book alternatives for themselves

---

* See the publicity stunts of the Fathers 4 Justice in Britain for a particularly vivid example of why a homemade Batman costume just doesn't cut it in real life.

† Specifically, it evokes the chevron on the chest of Miracleman.

‡ Editors' note: Elvis based his look—including his hair, sideburns, jumpsuit with short cape, and "Taking Care of Business in a Flash" logo—on Captain Marvel Jr. See Robby Reed's four-part

as the basis of their bolder stage personas. Just as Walter Kovacs branded himself "Rorschach" and covered his face with a black-and-white blot to close the door on his old life, so Terry Nelhams-Wright took on the name "Adam Faith"—with its Biblical connotations of belief and the creation of a brand new man—as part of his transformation into a TV star and teen idol. And as Bruce Wayne was inspired by a bat crashing through his window and adopted its name as a dark totem, so a British singer called Harry Webb took on "Cliff," for its towering evocations of rock music, and "Richard," as a tribute to his idol, Little Richard. Of course, Cliff Richard's group, the Shadows, was a guitar band rather than a crime-fighting team, but the importance of the origin story—the concept of choosing a new name, of baptism and rebirth—is as central to celebrity as it is to superhero culture.*

It was in late-1960s New York that the costumed heroes of comic books truly collided with their real-world counterparts. Warhol made himself into a distinctive brand, created a science fiction silver Factory, and surrounded himself with a clique of superstars. His followers, with alter egos like Ultra Violet, Billy Name, Ondine, Candy Darling, and the Velvet Underground, could have walked right out of Marvel comics. But the connections between costumed heroes and celebrities went further. Warhol and his contemporaries borrowed from superhero comics, enlarging panels to canvas size for gallery exhibition, and the comics borrowed back, marketing themselves as "authentic Pop Art." Warhol's crowd was even invited to the launch of the 1960s *Batman* TV show, and Warhol and German singer Nico dressed up as Robin and Batman for a 1967 *Esquire* shoot. Back in the UK, the Beatles disguised themselves as Sgt. Pepper's Lonely Hearts Club Band (it even sounds like a superhero group), and in 1975, Paul McCartney made explicit reference to Marvel Comics villains in the song "Magneto and Titanium Man."†

By the mid-1970s, of course, David Bowie's star had risen. Bowie had followed his own superhero-style origin story: Growing up in post-war London suburbia and possessed by the belief that he could be someone—or some*thing*—out of the ordinary, he ditched the dull name "Jones," re-christened himself after a type of knife (what could be more cutting edge?), and launched himself as a science fiction icon. In fact, a single persona wasn't enough for Bowie; he went through a host of incarnations. By 1975 he'd already killed off one larger-than-life character, Ziggy Stardust, and was moving through new masks, costumes, and names like a superhero on speed. The very idea of killing off his alien alter ego is a grand, pop-operatic statement suitable for a comic book cover—"Ziggy is DEAD! Call me...ALADDIN SANE!"

The 1970s rock band KISS was even more explicit in its debt to costumed heroes, and the debt was repaid when they and their on-stage alter egos—the Demon, the Starchild, the Space Ace, and the Catman—appeared in their own Marvel comic book

---

series, "The Secret Origins of Elvis and Captain Marvel Jr." (*Dial B for Blog*, http://www.dialbfor-blog.com/archives/85/).

* In the 1960s, Britain had its own code-named costumed heroines, too, in icons like Lulu and Twiggy.

† The song appears on the B-side to the Wings single "Venus and Mars/Rock Show."

in 1977. The back-and-forth relationship between comic books and popular culture continued when, three years later, Marvel created a new heroine to cash in on the disco craze. The new superhero, Dazzler, was planned as a cross-platform phenomenon, a comic book character who would also release records. In turn, the disco music style influenced long-running characters like Batman's sidekick, Robin: When the Boy Wonder grew up and, in a second re-birth, chose the new name Nightwing, he ditched the old-fashioned red and green costume for a midnight blue catsuit with a Dazzler-style disco collar (only a decade or so after they'd fallen out of fashion).

The interplay between music and comic books continued into the 1980s and 1990s. When a superhero character was "reborn" (i.e., rebooted for a new generation of readers), his new macho attitude was often signaled by a leather jacket, inspired by the previous decade's pop music pin-ups. For instance, the new teenage Superman of 1993* (slogan: "Don't ever call me SUPERBOY!") wore leathers over his costume and looked like a missing member from the 1980s boy-band Bros or George Michael at the start of his solo career.

British comic book writers were a little more knowing about the trend: creator Grant Morrison gave his home-grown superhero Zenith a pop career and showed him fuming at his pretty rivals Bros and A-ha, scorning Acid House music, and then selling out to the "baggy" Manchester fashions of the 1990s. Further examples from the decade emphasize the playful borrowings between pop music and superhero comics. Alan Moore's occult detective John Constantine was explicitly based on another rock star, Gordon Sumner, known to the world as Sting. John Smith's *The New Statesmen* depicted superheroes as gorgeous celebrities, prefiguring our current tendency to turn golden couples into brand names; Brangelina, TomKat, and Posh and Becks could be alternate versions of the comic book characters Bulleteer, Kitty Pryde, and Hawk and Dove.

Meanwhile, in the music industry, the origin stories continued, as ordinary boys and girls dreaming of stardom took on outlandish costumed identities. More than ever, young hopefuls transforming themselves into potential pop stars went through a process of superhero-style baptism like Bowie's, deliberately elevating themselves above the ordinary into something glittering, transcendent, and larger than life.

Take Paul Hewson, for instance, who grew up in an ordinary Dublin suburb, joined a rock band, and decided to take on a new identity. He could have gone for a version of the more modest stage personae of previous generations (like Cliff Richard and Adam Faith), but instead he adopted a stranger brand, "Bono Vox," and led a supergroup called U2. As with Rorschach and indeed Batman and Bowie, "Bono" seems to have taken over from the real person; rather than just a stage name, the persona has become the main identity. It's Bono, not Paul Hewson, who holds high-level discussions with politicians and popes. Like Rorschach and Batman, Bono wears a

---

* Editors' note: Following the "Death of Superman" event in 1992, DC Comics ran a year-long "Reign of Superman" story arc featuring four replacement supermen, one of whom was a 16-year-old clone genetically engineered to possess Superman's powers. Later on, after Superman had been resurrected, the character was rechristened Superboy.

mask—the wraparound shades constantly shielding his eyes—but he also needs the symbolic mask of his chosen name, and the larger-than-life persona it implies, even off stage. Tellingly, Bono also calls his closest bandmate "Edge," rather than David Evans; the alter ego, for both men, has become (to quote their own lyrics) even better than the real thing.*

Equally telling is the way Bono, like Bowie, has consistently invented new personae over the years. Already an iconic character, Bono disguised himself further onstage as "The Boy in the Box," "The Fly," "Mirror Ball Man," and "MacPhisto," each a new construction of props, costume, voice, and gesture. The ability to ditch a former identity and adopt a new one—to start afresh, with a new face and name—is one of the powers that real-life celebrities share with superheroes, and the liberating joy of rebirth, of recreation, of relaunching yourself under a new brand (whether "Rorschach," "Batman," "Bono," or "Bowie"), can clearly be addictive.†

The pop heroine of a new generation is of course Stefani Germanotta, better known as Lady Gaga; like sidekicks Kid Flash and Robin, she grew up learning from role models—drawing from rock stars Bowie, Madonna, and Queen's Freddie Mercury‡ [11]—before changing her name, adopting a costume (or ten), and starting her own career. She even has an origin story: when her producer texted "Lady Gaga" to her phone, she declared, "That's it. Don't ever call me Stefani again."

Lady Gaga is the closest thing we've got right now to a comic book superheroine, a living embodiment of the American dream that both Bruce Wayne and Clark Kent have embodied since the 1930s: The idea that anyone—especially someone from an immigrant background, like Superman himself—can dream big, work hard, and make it, even if "making it" means the construction of a whole new identity.

It may seem like a raw deal, a pale copy of superhero comics. Gaga doesn't patrol the city fighting crime, after all, any more than Bowie donned his Ziggy Stardust guise to protect the innocent and make the streets safer. (As a pop star turned political campaigner and philanthropist, Bono is, arguably, a rare exception.) There might be something super about giving yourself a new name and baptizing yourself as a star, but there's nothing obviously heroic in the process.

Not obviously, perhaps. But what our real-world costumed characters offer is the power of carnivalesque reinvention, which they hold out, as role models, to their followers. Lady Gaga modeled herself on the self-made stars of a previous generation, and just as Bowie, Madonna, and Freddie Mercury have inspired countless young people to find their own inner strength, to dress up and bravely parade even in the most conservative small towns and suburbs, so Gaga shows today's teenagers that it's just fine to be different—that being different, in fact, is a way of being special. It's a power.

The TV show *Glee* picked up on this idea in a recent storyline. Its main characters are all, in one way or another, misfits, social rejects, and outsiders—a pregnant

---

* "Even Better Than the Real Thing" is a single from U2's album *Achtung Baby*, released in 1992.
† Prince's renaming of himself in 1993 as a superhero-style sigil, an unpronounceable logo like the bat symbol, is an even more extreme example.
‡ Editors' note: Freddy Mercury's birth name was Farrokh Bulsara.

teenager, a young gay man, a student in a wheelchair, a football player who loves musical theater—brought together by their passion for song and dance. In a 2010 episode, they all dressed in either Gaga drag or KISS makeup and formed a united front—gay, straight, male, and female—against homophobic bullies who picked on one of their group for being different. Blocking a school corridor in their flamboyant masks, outfits, and makeup and facing down the burly football jocks, *Glee*'s misfits didn't look like losers; they looked like superstars. They looked like superheroes.

In comic books and pop celebrity, the origin story—the story of how Walter became Rorschach, of how Stefani became Gaga—is about gaining new confidence, ditching your old identity, and becoming someone new. Like superheroes, pop stars show us that a wimp, a persecuted loner, a nobody, can become a somebody. The science nerd can become a wise-cracking wall-crawler. The suburban dreamer, whether from London or Dublin, can dream out loud and conquer the world under a new name. This isn't just a conventional makeover, a sell-out to dominant ideals. The misfits don't become mainstream; they make their own style of strangeness big and bold. They dare the world to deal with them on their own terms, and they invite others to join them.

And if they can do it, we can, too. It doesn't have to happen on a global scale; we can do it on our own terms, ditching our old, weaker, shyer selves and becoming someone else, someone bigger, better, brighter, bolder...and someone who belongs. Gloriously decorated, disguised in their face paint and ornate dresses, *Glee*'s marginalized misfits weren't just new versions of their old selves; they were part of a team. They were part of something larger, pulling together to support each other, to defend the bullied and embrace the outsider, in the name of Gaga.

So our own pop icons don't stop locomotives, move faster than speeding bullets, or leap tall buildings in a single bound. But they offer a more important power. To people who feel they don't fit, they hold out the offer of belonging to a super-team where "misfit" is another world for "special," where being different from the norm is something to embrace and aspire to. They hold out the promise David Bowie made in 1977.

We could be heroes.

THREE

What is a Female Superhero?

Jennifer K. Stuller

Jennifer K. Stuller is a pop culture historian and critic, focusing on what popular culture can tell us about social mores, particularly regarding gender and sexuality in a given time or place. She is a contributor to *Critical Approaches to Comics: Theories and Methods* (Routledge, 2011) and editor of *Fan Phenomena and Buffy the Vampire Slayer* (Intellect, 2013). Her essay is based on her book, *Ink-Stained Amazons and Cinematic Warriors: Superwomen in Modern Mythology* (I.B. Tauris, 2010).

Some argue that a superhero must meet a particular set of criteria regarding origin, identity, supernatural powers, and costume in order to be defined as such. Yet for me, a superhero doesn't necessarily have to adhere to rigid genre rules to be considered superheroic. It is certainly useful to observe and utilize conventions when talking about a particular subject, but I have no interest in arguing over whether Batman's lack of superpowers and Buffy Summers's lack of costume render them technically "heroes," and not "*super*heroes."

As I asserted in my book, *Ink-Stained Amazons and Cinematic Warriors: Superwomen in Modern Mythology*, I believe a superhero is strong-willed, committed, resilient, and skilled. A superhero becomes super by surpassing the limits of the human body and mind, through rigorous training, an industrial accident, genetic mutation, advanced evolution, or being an alien. Sometimes a person is destined to be super. He or she can be prophesized and called to duty or created in a lab. A superhero can grace the pages of comics or be a warrior of the digital or silver screen.[1] She (or he) can be superheroic in any number of ways, including as a spy, a secret agent, an assassin, a costumed superhero, a detective, a witch, a reporter, a mentor, or even a sidekick.

A superhero story often borrows classic and archetypal themes from world mythology, and it can also involve the paranormal or fantastic. Superheroes are uniquely talented—some so much so that they become synonymous with their skill (think of Green Arrow and archery)—and they have a commitment to fighting for the greater good.[2] As Roz Kaveney writes in *Superheroes! Capes and Crusaders in Comics and Films*, "The mission is an important defining characteristic, as much so as [a superhero's] powers." Kaveney notes that people who lack the traditional powers associated with superheroes are still generally considered superheroic if they share a commitment to the superhero mission of fighting for "truth, justice, and the protection of the innocent."[3] So according to the most basic definition, a superhero might or might not have powers and might or might not wear a costume, but he or she must be committed to working for the greater good.

My work focuses specifically on female superheroes. While I'd rather we lived in a world in which we could just discuss heroes and not have to focus specifically on gender, cultural ideas of sex and gender are present in our fictional stories, intended or not. Because of this, the question I'm most interested in and feel most compelled to find answers to is, "What is a female superhero?" In fact, in my work I write about *superwomen*, a word I use interchangeably with the terms *superheroes*, *female heroes*, and *action heroines*. Lacking an element of the traditional genre criteria* (e.g., Buffy has a secret identity, superpowers, and an origin story but doesn't wear an iconic costume) doesn't make a character any less of a superhero to me.† We need to expand our ideas about what constitutes a female superhero, especially because women—no matter how kick-ass, capable, smart, or skilled they may be—are typically limited to the supporting roles of love interests, temptresses, and sidekicks and exist in relation to the male hero as the damsel in distress, kid sister or cousin, daughter, caretaker, or nurturer. Women, of course, can be these things, but we can also be more—so much more.

Because stories about superheroes can teach us about our socially appropriate roles (or, if we're savvy, how to subvert them), how we fit into our communities, and about our human potential, both terrible and great, it is the overwhelming focus on the male experience of heroism—and mostly white, heterosexual male heroism at that—that inspires my investigation of the female hero and her journey, challenges, accomplishments, and relationships, as well as how her experience of superheroism might be unique. This is not to suggest that her actions or journey are better, worse, more meaningful, more resonant, or more entertaining than those of her male counterparts—just that, for whatever reason, be it social or cultural influences or personal beliefs on the part of the creative team, they are different.

Thematically, the female experience of superheroism appears to differ most from that of men in its focus on collaboration, love, and mentorship, which prompts questions about whether the ways in which these ideas play out in the lives of superwomen express or are representative of something distinctly female or are indicative of limited ideas about femininity.

COLLABORATION

Female superheroes reject the "lone wolf" model of heroism that is typically favored by male protagonists—from Sam Spade to Superman to James Bond and so on—preferring instead to collaborate with and support those around them.‡ Often this collaboration is done with the assistance of a loving and supportive member of a family that the hero has created, rather than one linked by blood. The female character of Max Guevara on the television show *Dark Angel* (2002–2004) started out as a lone wolf,

---

* See Peter Coogan's *Superhero: Secret Origin of a Genre* for a thorough examination of the genre.
† Buffy Summers's choice of attire is addressed within the series itself, most notably in the fourth-season episode "The I in Team" (4.13). Buffy is allied with a covert military group, and when confronted over her choice not to wear the standard uniform, she responds, "Oh, you mean the camo and stuff. I thought about it, but on me it's gonna look all Private Benjamin. Don't worry, I've patrolled in this halter many times." Time and again Buffy proves that being a nonconformist makes her a better superhero. (And she doesn't need a costume.)
‡ With the exception of perhaps the X-Men, one rarely sees male superhero colleagues or allies referred to as family.

but her compassion and her fierce beliefs led her to liberate and protect her family of genetically altered but not necessarily genetically related "freaks." Similarly, the comic book version of Barbara Gordon (aka Batgirl and, later, Oracle) creates a family of mostly women in writer Gail Simone's run on the comic book series, *Birds of Prey*.

Buffy Summers, of the television series *Buffy the Vampire Slayer* (1997–2003), had her *Scoobies*—a group of friends who functioned as sidekicks. Additionally, the Slayer's origin story insists that there is a Slayer in every generation—one girl in all the world to fight evil. Buffy refuses to conform to the rigid isolation of the Slayer legacy and has friends, family, and romantic partnerships, and she literally shares her power with others—and she flourishes as no other Slayer before her because of this emotional connection with her allies.

As Sharon Ross observes in her contribution to 2004's *Action Chicks: New Images of Tough Women in Popular Culture*, whereas traditional heroes thrive on their individualism, modern female heroes grow as heroes because of their friends,[4] and women such as Buffy and her best friend, Willow, "are not heroes *for* other women so much as they are heroes *with* them."[5]

LOVE

The superwoman's story often emphasizes "love," be it romantic, filial, platonic, or as an ethic. This is not to suggest that male heroes aren't capable of love or do not work from a place of love. But it seems that love more often serves as narrative motivation for women characters, including, but not limited to, superheroes.

One example of this emphasis on love is the Amazon princess Wonder Woman and her inspirational and altruistic love for sisterhood, expressed in her interactions with women and children throughout her 70-year-long history in both illustrated and film incarnations. Another example can be found in the television series *Xena, Warrior Princess* (1995–2001), in which Xena, seeking redemption for past misdeeds, is transformed by the love of her traveling companion and friend (and, depending on your reading of the series, lover) Gabrielle, a farm girl turned warrior bard. The women share a deep affection for each other, and their mutual emotional, physical, and spiritual support facilitates their growth as heroes. Their love for each other pushes them to be better, and thus they become better heroes—they are, in effect, transformed by love. One of the many instances in which love is addressed in *Buffy the Vampire Slayer* comes when Buffy is afraid that the strength and resilience crucial to her role as an effective Slayer are making her hard inside and incapable of loving. On the suggestion of her mentor, she consults a spirit guide who assures Buffy that she's full of love, that love is her nature, and that it is "love" that will bring her to her gift.[6]

Why is love mentioned so often in the superwoman's journey, but not in the superman's? Does the use of love as narrative motivation or as the source of a female hero's strength reinforce traditionally gendered roles for women? Does a woman's love mean nurturing another, perhaps the hero, at the expense of her own heroism, or that love is in itself heroic? Is love a definitive component of a female superhero?

The answer to these questions is, "Perhaps." Again, consider Wonder Woman—the iconic female superhero—whose assets, strength, power, and mission were all rooted in love. Her creator, the eccentric psychologist William Moulton Marston, believed that comic book superheroes suffered from "blood-curdling masculinity" and that if he infused a female character with what he considered distinctly female traits such as maternal energy and sexual allure, it could change the world. Above all, Marston believed the character would effect these changes through her "loving authority." Though Wonder Woman's love was meant to influence both women and men, Marston's assertion that women's love made them better leaders than men (and that females were more capable of loving) was an essentialist suggestion. But the love expressed by a character such as Buffy has the power to *inspire*—and this difference, though subtle, is more egalitarian in its message. Women and men alike wield the power of love in the Buffy universe, from Buffy's sacrificing her life for that of her sister to Buffy's dear friend and partner in the fight against evil, Xander Harris, who asks himself in difficult situations, "What would Buffy do?" and in turn follows her example to save the world himself through an act of love.

MENTORSHIP

There are few examples of women mentoring superhero women.* Superwomen are almost always mentored by men—either fathers or father figures. Their mothers are absent or inconsequential. From Barbara Gordon (Batgirl) to Max Guevara (of the *Dark Angel* television series) to even the Powerpuff Girls, the lack of a maternal figure suggests that although women themselves perhaps draw their power from a place of love (and that such love is inherently feminine), when girls kick ass, it's because of the assistance, guidance, and teaching they receive from men. The absence of the mother figure reinforces the idea that heroism is masculine in nature and that female knowledge all too often has no value in the formation of a superwoman (though in superwomen, the learned masculine power is, of course, feminized through the emphasis on love).

SUPERWOMEN

So, what *is* a female superhero?

She is love, she is inspiration, she is vengeance; she is a mother, a daughter, a student, and a leader. She works for the good of others, though sometimes she's more concerned with achieving personal goals.

She can be sexy or sexualized, but she isn't necessarily defined by her sexuality. She can be an oppressive stereotype or an empowering icon—often she is simultaneously both. Above all, a female superhero, a *superwoman*, is complex and cannot be simply defined. This is why it's important to ask specifically, "What is a *female* superhero?"

---

* And yet occasionally we do see women mentoring young male heroes—for example, Sarah and John Connor of the *Terminator* franchise, or Lady Jessica and Paul "Muad'Dib" Atreides of *Dune*.

Keeping in mind the writers, artists, directors, actresses, and marketing departments who influence fictional characters, we must ask ourselves whether differences in the representations of male and female superheroes exaggerate or reflect cultural gender norms. What does it mean for a female hero to "use" her sexuality or have "love" be one of her gifts? Does an emphasis on love, compassion, and nurturance, or on sexuality, reinforce traditional roles for women? Or do superwomen subvert gender expectations? We find our answers on a case-by-case basis by evaluating representations and receptions of those that do exist, as well as by exploring our relationships to the characters that resonate with us. No one superwoman will be a hero to all.

But to me, a superwoman has the potential to inspire girls and women to stand up, be strong, support others, and, most important, believe in themselves.* Buffy Summers provides a profound example of this inspiration when she invites young potential Slayers to make a choice. She asks them to change their own destiny, to have power, to stand up, and to be strong. As a quintessential superwoman (she was trained by a man, she's collaborative, and love is her gift), she shares her power, and in doing so provides a model of heroism that is profound and inspirational in both fictional and real worlds.

NOTES

1. Stuller, Jennifer K. *Ink-Stained Amazons and Cinematic Warriors: Superwomen in Modern Mythology*. London/New York: I.B. Tauris, 2010.
2. Stuller, *Ink-Stained Amazons and Cinematic Warriors*, pp. 5–7.
3. Kaveney, Roz. *Superheroes! Capes and Crusaders in Comics and Films*. London/New York: I.B. Tauris, 2008, p. 4.
4. Ross, Sharon. " 'Tough Enough': Female Friendship and Heroism in *Xena* and *Buffy*." In *Action Chicks: New Images of Tough Women in Popular Culture*. Edited by Sherrie A. Inness. New York: Palgrave Macmillian, 2004, p. 231. Here she is referring to Xena and Gabrielle, from the series, *Xena, Warrior Princess*, as well as to Buffy Summers and Willow Rosenberg.
5. Ross, Sharon. " 'Tough Enough': Female Friendship and Heroism in *Xena* and *Buffy*." In *Action Chicks: New Images of Tough Women in Popular Culture*. Edited by Sherrie A. Inness. New York: Palgrave Macmillian, 2004, p. 232 (emphasis in original).
6. "Intervention," 5.18. *Buffy the Vampire Slayer*. Writer, Jane Espenson. Director, Michael Gershman. Original air date: April 24, 2001.

---

* This is the sort of role model boys and men have in relative abundance.

FOUR

Straddling a Boundary: The Superhero and the Incorporation of Difference

Clare Pitkethly

Clare Pitkethly's academic background is in comparative literature, culture, and communication. She writes and speaks about comics books and superheroes, including in her paper "Recruiting an Amazon: The Collision of Old World Ideology and New World Identity in Wonder Woman," published in *The Contemporary Comic Book Superhero*.

The superhero is, in simple terms, different—in some way *other*—fighting for a world that is *not quite* his or her own. Walking the line between two different worlds, the superhero is a go-between, with one foot on either side. In this way, the superhero straddles the boundary of a duality or an opposition and is simultaneously on one side and the other, incorporating both opposing sides. The superhero is split and is characterized by the tension of this contradiction: He or she is in some way paradoxical, and doesn't quite fit in.

The superhero is a figure of contradiction, a figure marked by an identity crisis: He or she belongs to two different worlds and is not entirely at home in either. To exemplify, Superman, a superhero often associated with American patriotism, presents a paradox that is particular to the United States' origins; in the words of Superman, "I'm an immigrant. Just like every *other* American."[1] Superman inhabits two different worlds, namely, the place of his origin, Krypton, and the land that he journeyed to, America. Superman is an alien who landed in America when the planet of his birth was destroyed. In the moments before his home world's destruction, his parents packed him into a small rocket and launched it in the hope that he could start a new life somewhere else. His capsule landed in an American cornfield, and he was adopted by a farmer and his wife.* Raised as an "all-American boy," he nonetheless finds himself to be different.[2] He develops superhuman abilities as a result of his alien physiology, and it is the yellow sun of Earth that fuels his unique superpowers. It is only as an *outsider* living on Earth that he is able to perform superhuman feats as Superman. A celebrated hero, he is regarded as "the best citizen of his society"; however, his superpowered superiority comes from the use of "alien trump cards."[3] Superman is simultaneously an American and a foreign alien, and it is this very duality that makes him a superhero.

Batman, like Superman, also straddles a boundary between two sides of an opposition, a contradiction that is best explained by Batman's butler, Alfred: "You chose as

---

* Editors' note: Superman's identification with Kansas originates with *Superman: The Movie* (1978), which placed Smallville in Kansas. Before then, Smallville had an undetermined location that ranged from the East Coast to the Midwest depending on the individual story.

your name 'the *Batman*.' I like to think you did so deliberately. As if you aspired to be *both*. Bat and man."[4] Batman incorporates both the human and the beast: "There's a *beast* Batman, in the depths of your soul."[5] He is characterized by the tension between the two, an antagonism that is made explicit in Darwyn Cooke's graphic novel *Batman: Ego* in a confrontation between Batman's two sides, as Bruce Wayne (Batman's alter ego) literally comes face to face with the beast within him. The *internal* split between the two halves of the character becomes *externalized*, or, in other words, one identity splits off from the other. In the altercation between the two, one side refuses to be dismissed by the other: "If you denounce me—if you try to jam me back into your subconscious—then I promise I will torment you until the day we die!"[6] The conclusion of the story is reached when the two halves agree to join forces and each side agrees to keep the other in check. By simultaneously incorporating *both sides* of an opposition, the character is able to appear at home in similarly opposing worlds. By the bright light of day he is Bruce Wayne, a civilized, well-mannered man of wealth, wearing dinner suits, attending fundraisers, and moving in the circles of Gotham City's most powerful and influential. By night, however, he is within another realm, a world that seems to be the mirror image of the former. It is under the cover of darkness that Batman crouches in the shadows waiting for his prey, namely, those who threaten the power and wealth of the other, civilized world. It is the very antagonism of these two opposing worlds, worlds "as different as night and day," that further characterizes Batman.[7] He is at home within both worlds—light and darkness, or civilization and madness—and is simultaneously in both at once.

Wonder Woman, who debuted in 1941, also incorporates an opposition, one that can be traced back to her creator, William Moulton Marston, and his intention of endowing her with "all the strength of a Superman plus all the allure of a good and beautiful woman."[8] Marston's characterization of Wonder Woman straddles the boundary of a gendered opposition, and his heroine adds "masculine strength to feminine tenderness," both of which become "combined in a single character."[9] This aspect of her character is most clearly evident in her initial comic book appearances from the time of World War II (an era of Rosie the Riveter and rapidly changing gender roles). The following example, featuring Wonder Woman's demure alter ego Diana Prince, demonstrates how the superheroine subverts this gendered boundary in front of a World War II–era audience:

Diana Prince: Wonder Woman asked me to move this piano—ugh—unh—oh-h-h! It's too heavy for me!
Audience: Ha! Ha! Whe-ee-ew! Get a man! Get Wonder Woman![10]

In the above example, the Wonder Woman becomes equivalent to a man, or, simply put, she becomes different from other women.[11] The superheroine was born on a hidden island inhabited only by (female) Amazons, and she then embarked on a journey to "the world of men,"[12] a term Marston frequently used when referring to America. Marston's comics associate her homeland, Paradise Island, with "love and justice," while the "tortured, upside-down world of men" provides a distinct contrast.[13] One is the inverse of the other, and Wonder Woman becomes marked by the conflict of opposites as she simultaneously embraces both—opposing—worlds.

Superman, Batman, and Wonder Woman each incorporate an *otherness*, and their respective superpowers are the result of this very difference. Their powers are linked to other realms—the alien planet Krypton or the female-only Paradise Island—or, in the case of Batman, a savage or bestial *otherness*. This incorporation of difference—or, more directly, of both sides of an opposition—is not limited to DC's "Big Three" (Superman, Batman, and Wonder Woman). The same logical model can be applied more broadly to other superheroes. For instance, the alien Martian Manhunter and the oceanic Aquaman are further examples of superheroes who straddle the boundary between American and foreigner (or alien). Like Batman, many superheroes gain their particular superpowers by straddling the boundary between human and beast, such as Wolverine, Spider-Man, Hawkman, and Animal Man.*

As with Wonder Woman, superhero comics frequently demonstrate the empowerment of those who have traditionally been marginalized; in this sense, such superheroes straddle the division between being denied power and having power. For instance, the Green Arrow operates at the junction between the wealthy and the working class, and the ostracized social misfits in the X-Men and in the Doom Patrol become marginalized as a result of their very superpowers. Superheroes derive their powers by subverting boundaries, by incorporating difference, and by becoming somehow *other*, for instance, by tapping into the strange otherworldliness of magic (the magician Zatanna), nature (the plant-like Swamp Thing), or the divine (Thor).† Monstrous superheroes such as the Hulk demonstrate the incorporation of an *otherness* associated with the grotesque.

The division between large and small is straddled by size-shifting superheroes who subvert physical boundaries, such as the Atom and Giant Man; the solid and the fluid meet in the shape-changing Plastic Man; and the transition between superhuman speed and a slower moving human temporality is made by the Flash, among others.‡

---

* Editors' note: There are two versions of Hawkman. The first debuted in 1940 and is archeologist Carter Hall, secretly a reincarnation of an ancient Egyptian prince, Khufu, who wears hawk wings made of an anti-gravity metal and a hawk mask. The second Hawkman, from the 1960s, is Katar Hol, a police officer from the planet Thanagar who fights crime on Earth and similarly wears anti-gravity hawk wings and a hawk mask. Like Captain America, as noted elsewhere in the chapter, the original Hawkman also crosses temporal boundaries, and the second Hawkman, like Superman, is an alien and crosses the citizen/foreigner boundary as well. Animal Man has the power to borrow the abilities of nearby animals.

† Zatanna is a magician who uses her magical abilities to fight crime. Swamp Thing was originally a scientist who was caught in a bomb explosion and took on the properties of the swamp his body fell into. Later it was revealed that the explosion actually killed the scientist and his consciousness was revived in the plant body of an earth elemental. Swamp Thing has been featured in a number of low-budget films and television series.

‡ Fluidly changing, each size-shifting superhero is simultaneously larger than he was and smaller than he will be. The Atom has the ability to shrink to subatomic size, but he usually operates at about a six-inch height. Giant Man can increase his height to about 60 feet. Plastic Man is "plastic"

Straddling the boundary between humanity and technology, Iron Man and Steel combine both man and machine.* Part human and part superpowered armor, they possess a superhero status that is the result of the simultaneity of the two. In a somewhat similar fashion, Captain America was initially created to be a superpowered weapon in World War II. His superpowers were induced by a synthetic serum, and he fuses humanity with a chemically enhanced excess (or perhaps with the lethality of a chemical weapon).

Incorporating both sides of an opposition, the superhero embodies a paradox, or, in other words, he becomes unsure of exactly what he actually *is*. The Swamp Thing demonstrates this confusion succinctly: "Am I a plant that dreams he is a man? Or a man who dreams he is a plant?"[14] As the superhero walks the line of a boundary, his or her identity becomes strangely contradictory, as he or she incorporates two different sides, and it is the very simultaneity of both sides within the character that gives the superhero his or her extraordinary superpowers. To clarify using the words of Superman, "Conflict and consequence . . . ultimately leads to *growth*."[15] Straddling the boundary between the two sides of a logical opposition, the superhero incorporates a paradox or a contradiction, and it is the dynamic tension that results from this split that makes him or her *super*human.[†]

NOTES

1. Joe Casey and Derec Aucoin, *Adventures of Superman* #613, April 2003. New York: DC Comics, p. 11.
2. Garth Ennis and John McCrea, *Hitman* #34, February 1999. New York: DC Comics, p. 13.
3. Steven T. Seagle and Teddy H. Kristiansen, *It's a Bird...*, May 2004. New York: Vertigo (DC Comics), p. 49.
4. Michael Green and Denys B. Cowan, *Batman Confidential* #8, October 2007. New York: DC Comics, p. 21.
5. John Marc DeMatteis and Mark Pajarillo, *JLA* #35, November 1999. New York: DC Comics, p. 38.
6. Darwyn Cooke, *Batman: Ego*. New York: DC Comics, 2000, p. 50.
7. Doug Moench and Barry Kitson, *Batman: Legends of the Dark Knight* #147, November 2001. New York: DC Comics, p. 17.
8. William Moulton Marston. (1944). "Why 100,000,000 Americans Read Comics." *The American Scholar,* **13**(1), pp. 42–43.
9. Marston, "Why 100,000,000 Americans Read Comics," pp. 43, 44.
10. Charles Moulton [William Moulton Marston] and Harry G. Peter, *Wonder Woman* #6, Fall 1943. New York: DC Comics, p. 2a.

---

in the original sense of the word—he can reshape his body into any form. The Flash has the superpower of super speed.

* Steel wears a superpowered suit of armor, like Iron Man.

† In an interesting parallel, this same structure characterizes Nietzsche's "superman." It is the conflict of opposing forces *within* the superman (namely, the Apollonian and the Dionysian) that instigates his growth or his superiority.

11. Charles Moulton [William Moulton Marston] and Harry G. Peter, *Sensation Comics* #3, March 1942. New York: DC Comics, p. 5.

12. Charles Moulton [William Moulton Marston] and Harry G. Peter, *Sensation Comics* #7, July 1942. New York: DC Comics, p. 1.

13. Charles Moulton [William Moulton Marston] and Harry G. Peter, *Sensation Comics* #2, February 1942. New York: DC Comics, p. 1.

14. Nancy A. Collins and Scot Eaton, *Swamp Thing* #129, March 1993. New York: Vertigo (DC Comics), p. 12.

15. Joseph Kelly and Jose Angel Cano Lopez, *Action Comics* #782, October 2001. New York: DC Comics, p. 19. (The italics are mine.)

FIVE

Save the Day

A. David Lewis

A. David Lewis holds a Ph.D. specializing in Religion & Literature from Boston University, where he founded the School of Theology Library's Religion and Graphica Collection. He both teaches about and writes graphic novels, including *The Lone and Level Sands* and *Some New Kind of Slaughter*. His essay below builds on ideas he put forth in "Superman Graveside" from the anthology *Graven Images: Religion in Comic Books and Graphic Novels*.

THE ESSENTIAL, SECRET SUPERPOWER

There is one superpower that *all* superheroes have, whether they know it or not.

Before we explore this one surprising power, let's take a quick trip to the local comic book store circa May 2007. Among the items we might notice there are leftover gratis comics from the annual Free Comic Book Day, all sorts of tie-in merchandise to the *Spider-Man 3* movie, an impressive number of small press and non-superhero works like *Mouse Guard* or *Naruto*, and several comic books memorializing the death of Captain America.

Yes, in May 2007, Captain America was thought dead. So, too, were Superboy in May 2006, Wonder Girl in May 2005, the Thing in May 2004, Green Lantern in May 2003, and so forth. One does not need to know any of these characters specifically to grapple with the following fact: by May 2007, they had all returned from the dead, remarkably. (Captain America did the same by 2010, so don't fear.)

What should be shocking is that these deaths and, later, the almost inevitable returns are *not* shocking. Somehow, they have become commonplace for the superhero. In that comic shop in May 2007, an explanation for what one online columnist called superheroes' "revolving door of death"* can be found on a large promotional poster. The advertisement is for a major superhero series that will be coming out in the next year, *Final Crisis*. The poster shows superheroes such as Superman, Batman, Wonder Woman, and the Flash posed in dark silhouettes, and the tagline promoting the upcoming series reads, "Heroes die. Legends live forever."

Precisely: *heroes die, but legends live forever*—that is, heroes *can* die, but there is a class above the hero, that of the legendary *super*hero, whose members can bypass permanent death. This draws a sharp distinction between the *hero* and the *superhero*, and that is a subtle yet important difference. Although the distinction often gets overlooked or simply glossed over, a superhero, in fact, has qualities that make him or her different from (though not necessarily superior to) the modern Western understanding of a

---

* A term popularized by the online comic book commentary site *The Quarter Bin*, http://community.fortunecity.ws/tatooine/niven/142/revolvin/rdmaster.html

hero, and the reverse is certainly true. When heroes die, they stay dead; when super-heroes die, they may well come back from the dead.

In short, a superhero is a super-empowered hero, one who not only risks death to defend others but has the ability to beat it as well. This ability to evade permanent death is the unspoken, widespread power wielded by superheroes, and it is practically definitional. It finds its source, where else, but in the origin of the superhero genre and the American cultural consciousness.

THE GROWING PERIL

Plenty of people have argued about whether Superman was the first superhero; regardless, his arrival in the late 1930s certainly solidified the mold by breaking an old one. Masked men with incredible talents were already a staple of American fiction on the radio, on the screen, and in the low-cost pulp magazines. These "pulp heroes" such as Doc Savage,* The Shadow,† Tarzan, and Zorro bore a definite resemblance to their superhero siblings, but Superman and his comics allies moved audiences into a new genre. Readers were becoming enthralled with these skintight-costumed vigilantes who could do things far, far beyond the capabilities of those in even peak human con-dition. The scales shifted from pulp stories in which most of the protagonists exhibited abilities that someone with years of extensive and dedicated training could master to stories in which these gifts often defied natural physics. Giving a character superhu-man speed was no longer sloppy writing, and flight was more than a flight of fancy. Consumers welcomed the utterly fantastic.

The creation of the superhero was the 1930s' response to morality, but not yet to mortality. Several comics scholars have commented on the range of possible factors in this extraordinary time that led to the superhero. Many of them—from immigration to the Depression, from racism to classism, from world affairs to local strife—can be boiled down to America negotiating a revised morality. How should outsiders be treated? How does our society work? What is justice? Readers of all ages, but espe-cially juveniles, would escape to superhero adventures to have these issues addressed. The basic Clark Kent/Superman dualism has at its core this sense of the helpless being both aided by and equal to the all-powerful, instead of dominated by them. In fact, in his exploration of Jewish immigrants and the rise of the superhero, *Disguised as Clark Kent: Jews, Comics, and the Creation of the Superhero* (Continuum, 2007), author Danny Fingeroth specifically points out that the drive for rightfulness exhibited by Superman might have come from a seminal injustice dealt to his co-creator, Jerry Siegel. As a youth, Siegel's father, a humble store owner, was gunned down by a robber who was never caught. The world could be perceived as a very unfair place if one didn't believe in the balance that could be provided by superheroes.

---

* Editors' note: Doc Savage is Clark Savage, Jr., a pulp adventurer who is also a scientist and physician, among other occupations. He has trained his keen abilities since he was an infant. The portrayal of Doc Savage influenced the depiction, and possibly the creation, of Superman.
† Editors' note: The Shadow is a dark pulp vigilante who debuted in 1931. He is often depicted as having the power to "cloud men's minds" in order to be invisible.

The superhero originated as the popular American response to injustice, poverty, and situations beyond one's control. That response started by addressing everyday criminals, grew to encompass social ills (e.g., orphans, malnutrition, organized crime), and then was taken global with the outbreak of World War II. For all the valiant troops who fell, superheroes soldiered on, unbeatable and inspiring; again, here is the difference between heroism, remarkably displayed by the American armed forces, and superheroism, which cannot be expected of mortal men, fictional or otherwise. In the 1950s, as the culture's fears grew (of communism, of nuclear war, of race war, of terrorism, of pandemic, etc.), superheroes' capacities to defend us grew, too. In less than a century, the genre had become an endless response to the ultimate situation beyond one's control: dying.

Before returning to our present in 2013 and the ugliness of modern death,* let's say one more thing about this "endless" response, specifically, the serial nature of superheroes' original medium, comics. Whether in comic strips in the newspaper or comic books on the newsstand, superheroes originated and make their home in visual stories that always ask, *What's next?* One panel alone rarely ever tells the whole story. Sequentiality—one panel followed by another followed by another—is required of most comics storytelling (thus their more sophisticated name, "sequential art").† Superheroes have this idea of sequence built into their narrative DNA, as it were. After one panel comes another panel, after one page comes another page, after one adventure comes another adventure. The last page is never the *last* page, because another installment is soon to come in superheroes' never-ending quest for justice. Even if read critically as agents of hegemony, enforcers of normalcy, or upholders of the status quo, their work is still never done. We expect superheroes to always continue.

This endless superhero‡ has come to represent two great American themes. First, it reflects our denial of death. While an instinct for self-preservation is readily found in the animal kingdom, human cognition lifts it to a new peak, and our psyches can oftentimes create a complex out of it. That is the central message of cultural anthropologist Ernest Becker's book *The Denial of Death*: we set up mental blocks to

---

* Although there has been improvement socially since its original publication, Jessica Mitford's *The American Way of Death* details the 20th-century trend of hiding death, shutting away the elderly, and clandestinely hospitalizing the sick. Whereas the passing of a loved one used to be something that took place at home and in the presence of family, over time it has become, according to Mitford's report, largely profane and something to be hidden.

† Editors' note: Scott McCloud, in *Understanding Comics*, defines comics as "juxtaposed pictorial images in deliberate sequence," which can be shortened to "sequential art" (p. 9).

‡ Neil Gaiman fans shouldn't confuse this mention of the "endless" with his pantheon of capital-E "Endless" characters including the titular Sandman. In fact, although superheroes do appear in his work, *The Sandman* is not a superhero story. It is made very clear by the series conclusion that characters in that series can and do die. Compare this sentiment to the work of Gaiman's comics mentor Alan Moore and his superhero opus *Watchmen*: unlike Gaiman's Endless, Moore's endless Doctor Manhattan says as his final words, "Nothing ever ends." (Yet, the book *does*—unless it's adapted into a movie, spun off into sequels, sold as a role-playing game, etc.)

keep us from fully acknowledging death, and we reward those who risk their own well-being to shield us from it by calling them heroes—people who would risk all or part of their person so that we are not required to. However, the denial of death is rooted deeper in our minds, suggests Becker, oftentimes compelling the illusion that it will always be *others* who face death, not *us*. Wars happen far away,* poverty is another person's affair, and cholesterol won't catch us! Usually, people who face these issues when they are not required to are, rightly, called heroes. They expend themselves, risk their livelihoods (their time, their effort, and their energies, if not literally their lives), for others. Perhaps for most of us, heroism can be left for others to undertake; we would rather experience heroism vicariously, if at all—in our entertainment, identifying either with the superheroes who *can* deny death or the people they tirelessly protect.

In addition to a denial of death, the second theme superheroes reflect is our habit of seeing our lives as stories, as narrative. For instance, one of the pinnacles of English literature in the 20th century is James Joyce's *Ulysses*,† which essentially just creates a narrative of a standard Dublin day. We do this all the time: our vacations take on a narrative arc, our romantic dates become stories, and even a day at the office has a discernable beginning-middle-and-end structure. One way people conceptualize their lives and, in particular, give them meaning in the face of finitude is by making them into stories. Superhero stories reinforce this tendency. That is, some comics and movies seem to recognize this trend of "endless" superheroing and move beyond heroism and death to recenter the narrative on storytelling. Superheroes transcend death because stories do; Robin Hood quests so long as his tale is told, Tinkerbell lives as long as we believe, and remember the Alamo! If we become part of a story—if an albeit fictional superhero affects our lives in a way that inspires, encourages, or even entertains—then some portion of us always lives on. Superheroes have become our stories of choice not only for staving off death, but also for pursuing immortality.

THE NEVER-ENDING BATTLE

So, a lot of generalities were just tossed about above; let's talk facts now.

---

* It would be disingenuous, of course, not to note how rocked the American consciousness was by September 11, 2001, when our vulnerabilities were horrifically revealed. Like Pearl Harbor, it caused a trauma for the nation and, as an echo, a reevaluation of the American superhero in its wake. See my article "The Militarism of American Superheroes after 9/11" in *Comic Books and American Cultural History: An Anthology* (Bloomsbury, 2012).

† Notably, it was serialized also, as was much of English literature in the ramp up to the superhero. Yet these novels' final forms are commonly aimed at a codex, a book, whereas—until the late 20th century—the primary form of the superhero story was the monthly serial pamphlet. In contrast to a novel's preexistence in serialized form, the comic book more closely resembles an epic poem like *The Odyssey* (a very different Ulysses!), with oral cantos that suggest no end; when the poem does finish, though, characters like Odysseus are compelled to return to journeying rather than die at home.

When it comes to a superhero's prosocial mission,* it is not about changing society but about maintaining it, and his own place and role in it. Oftentimes, the character himself (or herself) is not aware of this ulterior motive. Take, for instance, the "Death of Superman" in 1992. It was covered in *Newsweek*, in *USA Today*, and in numerous other mainstream periodicals: Superman died. Of course, he would be back in action within a year—revived by alien Kryptonian technology or some such bit of technowizardry—but his absence caused an immediate void, which was filled by four competing supermen. Their quartet of stories filled the year-long "World Without Superman" arc and allowed a long-haired, refocused Man of Steel to return to action. In the end, the net result for the comic was next to nothing, except phenomenal sales, a few new supporting characters, and a reinvigorated Superman. More specifically, readers got *their* Superman, a new vision of the 60-year-old character.

As a superhero maintains society and maintains himself, comics creators are given the opportunity to recreate him through such rebirths. "The Death of Superman" was never about his being or remaining dead; it was about how he would return. Re-read that last sentence. It isn't saying *in what manner* he would return but instead *in what form* he would return, *who he would be* upon his return. When Superman came back, he was a tad hipper, a bit more relatable, and maybe a little wiser from the experience. He was refreshed. The trick here was that he had changed without aging, progressed without degrading. This trick is one that Superman's writers have been playing for years, and big brains like Umberto Eco have noticed it before. As far back as 1972, Eco wrote in his essay "The Myth of Superman" that we *know* Superman cannot die; he is not Superman if he does. In his words, Superman cannot be "consumed" but must appear to be. He has to change without changing, and this can be accomplished, paradoxically, through his dying and coming back new and improved. DC Comics did it in 1994,† as they did again in 2005,‡ as they had done before in 1986,§ just to name a few occasions.

Killing and resurrecting the superhero makes him transgenerational by recreating him. For a while, it was enough to have a character's identity bestowed on a younger inheritor, in a passing of the mantle. The Green Lantern created in 1940 did not have to die in order for a new Green Lantern, an entirely different man, to arise in 1959.** The same proverbial passing of the torch took place between the

---

* Editors' note: Peter Coogan defines the superhero's mission as prosocial and selfless, "which means that his fight against evil must fit in with the existing, professed mores of society and must not be intended to benefit or further his own agenda" (*The Secret Identity of the Superhero*, Austin, TX: Monkey Brain Books, 2006, p. 31).

† The series *Zero Hero: Crisis in Time* brought heroes back to the dawn of all creation only to have it all unfold again with some slightly different, streamlined details.

‡ The *Infinite Crisis* series reintroduced a multiplicity of realities—52, to be exact—and the resurrection of various characters due to an alternate Superman committing violence against the delicate walls of reality.

§ *Crisis on Infinite Earths* collapsed all the parallel universes and publishing histories associated with DC Comics into one comprehensive world.

** That's Alan Scott and Hal Jordan.

Flash of 1940 and the Flash of 1956. That is, over time, the old versions of superheroes were replaced by the publishers with newer, more contemporary versions, usually with updated costumes and new secret identities, as occurred with both Green Lantern and the Flash. Alternatively, some younger men did take up the name of a fallen superhero, like the Blue Beetle or the Human Torch. And there was always the old soap opera trick of a superhero not really being dead, such as the hibernating Captain America* or the time-lost Captain America† or, heck, the "he was an imposter all along" Captain America.‡ Don't get the mistaken impression that Captain America is the problem. At some point in most characters' decades-long publishing histories, they have each been recreated in some manner.§ Since the "Death of Superman" storyline, characters have been coming back directly from the dead, from the hereafter, in order to be made new again. And, like the shift from peak-human pulp heroes to more-than-human superheroes, readers have accepted it.

Being regarded as a superhero is enough to bring one back from the dead, even if a character does not exhibit all of the traditional superhero conventions. For the superhero, powers famously demand everyday responsibility but also bind one to endless, living responsibility. (Actually, never being allowed to die could be something of a curse, if one chose to look at it that way.**) But even without superhuman powers, if one accepts the responsibilities of a superhero, one might be bound to this existence just the same. That's right: even superpowers are optional in order for someone to be a superhero. Take, for instance, two archers, Green Arrow and Hawkeye. Both are normal men and incredibly accurate archers, and both, coincidentally, died in aircraft explosions. One of them would, through a friend's cosmic powers, be brought back as a soulless husk as his essence in Heaven was being cajoled to return (Green Arrow); the other would be resurrected *twice* thanks to a former ally's reshuffling of all reality (Hawkeye). On one hand, these men are very fortunate to have such compatriots. On the other hand, they demonstrate the awesomeness of this pervasive superhero

---

* The Avengers found Captain America, thought to have been killed at the end of World War II, in suspended animation within a block of ice in *Avengers* #4.

† Captain America's assassination proved to be instead his being shunted through time in the *Captain America: Reborn* series.

‡ It was later determined that the Captain Americas who served following World War II and until the Avengers' discovery were not the original one but replacements. See *What If?* #4 and *Captain America* #155.

§ Prime examples of a "reboot," wherein a publishing history is selectively revised and tailored, include *Crisis on Infinite Earths*, *Heroes Reborn*, *Unity 2000*, and *Infinite Crisis*, to name a few. Some would note that most superhero publishing universes have been recreated at least once, if not more.

** Comics readers can think here of the comedic, third-tier superhero Mister Immortal and his sole ability to recover from any fatality. More seriously, characters such as Wolverine, Resurrection Man, or even Superman himself in the graphic novel *Where Is Thy Sting?* have had to face the possible horror of never passing on.

convention—it is as though you know you have really made it as a superhero if you *cannot* die.

THE SPECTER OF DEATH

Mortality remains present in a superhero's life, but it threatens those around the super-hero, not the character himself. The superhero usually has some tie to a family mem-ber or loved one who has died, is threatened with death, or both.* With the exception of some very peculiar characters,† superheroes cannot know that they are endless, or all the drama and righteousness of their stories would be drained. Their lives would be rather absurd. In order for mortality to be *perceived* as a threat (thereby making a superhero still a hero by definition), the superhero must also be tied to the shadow of death. Whereas he or she might personally escape it, there is usually a dear one who cannot or will not. Peter Parker, the spectacular Spider-Man, has lost his Uncle Ben and worries constantly about the frailty of his only surviving relative Aunt May, even though Peter himself engages in incredibly high-risk behaviors. Batman and Superman would not be the crusaders they are if not for their orphanhoods, both Iron Man and Captain America are indebted to the early sacrifices of a mentor figure,‡ and even anti-hero killing machines like the Punisher and Wolverine have the murder of loved ones fueling their rage.

This "immunity" to permanent death is not a fearlessness of death, as death still affects others and may splash on the superhero himself. It creates the *appearance* of a superhero's mortality and keeps it present in his consciousness. Without the inclusion of this perceived threat of mortality in the superhero's origin, the concept of hero-ism—and, thus, superheroism—fails. Therefore, any superhero's likely return must be muddied by his or her loved ones' failure to return.

Often, it is the slain character who motivates the superhero and catalyzes his career as a secular savior. Don't misunderstand my use of the word *savior*; it is not synonymous with *messiah* and its typical religious connotations here. Successful superheroes look to uphold and to safeguard. Therefore, they are, in a literal sense, saviors—repositories who save the structure and the story of an individual like a living hard drive might. When Captain America was first revived from his World War II suspended animation

---

* Though the pronouns *he* and *himself* have been used throughout the chapter, what is true for the male superhero is generally true for the superheroine. However, with regard to gender, it would seem that the women in a superhero's life prove to be especially—perhaps misogynistically—sus-ceptible to harm. See Gail Simone's *Women in Refrigerators* (March 1999) (http://lby3.com/wir/).

† At various points in their publishing histories and under the pens of certain writers, characters such as The Psycho-Pirate, Animal Man, She-Hulk, Doctor Thirteen, Howard the Duck, and others have been made aware of their fictionality and, thus, their potential endlessness.

‡ For Iron Man, it was Professor Ho Yinsen, his fellow captive, who allowed himself to be killed in order that Iron Man might rise. For Captain America, it was also a professor, Abraham Erskine, whose death left young Steve Rogers as his only successful super-soldier.

in the 1960s, he pledged to continue fighting the good fight in honor of his lost partner Bucky. Where Captain America's story went, so, too, would Bucky (until Bucky got reanimated, too, albeit much, much later.) When a mantle is passed, such as in the case of the previously mentioned Green Lanterns and Flashes, so is the responsibility for shouldering the memories of others, living and dead. In fact, the cosmic character Nova is empowered as the last surviving member of the Nova Corps, entrusted with honoring the legacies of the slain members.

If superheroes as "savior hard drives" feels like too much of a stretch, take a moment to consider how often this concept comes up both in the superhero stories and in the industry that publishes them. In both fiction and fact, saving the memory and the presence of a person is vitally important for the genre. Team headquarters are filled with mega-databases of known allies, adversaries, alien races, power evaluations, histories, and so forth. These superteams behave like the ultimate comics collectors, amassing every piece of data that they can. Moreover—and more telling—these team headquarters often feature virtual assistants and protection systems with personalities. In one comic book reality, the Avengers have their loyal manservant Jarvis to aid them, while in another version of the Avengers, Jarvis is a sort of monitoring computer program (of the type seen in the *Iron Man* films). When the half-human superhero Cyborg sustains injuries too grievous for his physical body to endure, his consciousness is "downloaded" into a separate container. Similar circumstances have befallen other superheroes*; in many cases their consciousness or program becomes part of a superteam's base of operations. Said more plainly, the superheroes' homes often feature digitally collected personalities. We can read this form of preservation as one expression of superheroes' narrative collection of character stories.

The second expression of this narrative salvation is also suggested in the behavior of superheroes' writers, artists, and creators. Perhaps it is a lingering effect from the supposed ignominy of working in this trash medium circa the 1930s, but contemporary comics creators are now tremendously conscious of their predecessors and their pioneering work. Further, those who could have been ground under the corporate heel, such as Superman co-creators Siegel and Joe Shuster or Batman co-creator Bill Finger, have been championed through the legal system and in the court of public opinion by the generations of young minds they cultivated. Superhero writers and artists, if not their characters, sense the unendingness of superheroes and act on that shared impulse in the form of legacy. They, too, will die someday and perhaps live on only in the stories they have imparted to their inheritors.

THE SUPERHEROES' POPULAR MORTALITY

Our superheroes have no end, a function of both our national need (i.e., denial of death) and the serial nature of the comics medium. Like our country, our superheroes attempt to be both new and old simultaneously; they have the history and endurance

---

* Editors' note: Examples include the Doom Patrol's Robotman, the android Jocasta, the synthezoid Vision, and the mystic Obsidian.

of their past coupled with the opportunity to be reinvented continually by successive generations. The superhero says that we will endure, in some form or another. Right now, creators aware of this trend suggest that our heroes and our society will continue to survive as stories and as information. Both the fear and the denial of death are playing out in the popular superhero genre weekly, but almost without comment.

RECOMMENDED READING LIST

Ernest Becker. *The Denial of Death*. New York: Free Press, 1997.

Umberto Eco. "The Myth of Superman." *A Comics Studies Reader*. Jackson, MS: University of Mississippi Press, 2009.

A. David Lewis. "Superman Graveside." *Religion in Comic Books and Graphic Novels*. New York: Continuum International Publishing, 2010.

Grant Morrison. *Animal Man: Deus Ex Machina*. New York: Vertigo, 2003.

Grant Morrison. *Final Crisis*. New York: DC Comics, 2010.

Context, Culture, and the Problem of Definition

Powers and mission aren't the only elements that define a superhero or help us to identify one (or to identify with one). In addition to having a unique costume and appearance, each superhero is embedded both in his or her culture—the culture of the fictional world—and in our culture. A superhero's actions take place in context, and we experience them in our own contexts. The essays in this section explore the role that context, culture, and costume play in defining a superhero and creating the genre—or even whether it might be an impossible task to attempt to define these things.

SIX

Superheroes and the Modern(ist) Age

Alex Boney

Alex Boney began writing about comics during his graduate studies at The Ohio State University. He is a regular presenter at the Comic Arts Conference in San Diego and a regular contributor to industry publications such as *Back Issue!* He is currently an editor at Hallmark in Kansas City, MO, and he teaches classes on American literature and comics at the University of Central Missouri. His primary interest lies in superhero comics of the 1940s, but he has a soft spot for The Question, Power Girl, and Martian Manhunter.

The superhero is many things to many people of (and in) many ages. The perception of the genre has changed dramatically in the past three decades as superheroes have risen to greater prominence in popular culture and media. But at his core, the superhero is—and always has been—a response to the rapid, dizzying forces of early 20th century modernism. The origins of comics *as a medium* can be tied directly to developments in various print and visual media. The origins of superheroes *as a genre*, however, are rooted deeply in the wider cultural forces of the modern age. The first few decades of the 20th century were marked in America by rapid industrial growth, a shift from rural life to urban life, and worldwide war. Between the wars, Americans experienced a decade of economic boom that collapsed as the 1920s turned to the 1930s. Albert Einstein's theory of relativity and Heisenberg's uncertainty principle added to a general sense of unease that began to deflate and complicate supposedly stable notions such as "truth" and "honor." The scientific theories of relativity and uncertainty were, of course, not limited to time, space, and physics. Many early psychoanalysts and philosophers applied the idea of relativity to the human mind and to the very human concepts of justice, morality, and self.

The disillusionment that followed World War I brought this internal relativity to greater prominence. In response, American novelists created a series of protagonists who were morally confused, highly skeptical of abstract notions such as truth and justice, and prone to Hamlet-like introspection and self-destruction. The only norm in early 20th century America was that of constant flux, and many writers found a way to reflect the resulting instability and uncertainty in their fiction. Much like literary protagonists such as F. Scott Fitzgerald's Jay Gatsby, John Steinbeck's Tom Joad, and Ernest Hemingway's Frederick Henry, superheroes such as Superman, Batman, Starman, and the Flash were larger-than-life characters who struggled for order and meaning in a world mired in chaos, corruption, and moral uncertainty. Unlike their more introspective contemporaries, though, superheroes presented more proactive ways to cope with and respond to such a new and vibrant world.

In the early 20th century, the primary locus of power and energy was the city—a relatively new landscape that drastically transformed the social and geographical makeup of America.* As a new cultural force, the urban environment inspired both fear and awe. Many artists of the modern age accepted the city as a necessary aspect of human evolution. A group of artists calling themselves the Futurists issued a manifesto in 1909 that called for the embrace of "the city as a visual symbol of the new."[1] Many European and American architects and visual artists (such as Umberto Boccioni, Gino Severini, Mario Chiatonne, and even Georgia O'Keefe) agreed with the Futurists' aesthetic and celebrated the city in their work. Some of the most important European writers of the modernist period reflected the new urban dynamic by setting their novels in major capitals. Virginia Woolf's *Mrs. Dalloway*, James Joyce's *Ulysses*, and Marcel Proust's *Swann's Way* are all city novels. Even Batman and Robin were awestruck when they visited the New York World's Fair in 1940. As they wandered through the fair, they glanced around and marveled at the architectural wonders that surrounded them.[2] Like the Chicago Exhibition of 1893, the 1940 New York World's Fair represented the industrial and technological achievements of a country firmly ensconced in the forces—especially the urban forces—of modernity.

Like their European counterparts, many American modernists turned to the city to explain their rapidly changing world. And like the Europeans, American writers treated the city with a healthy dose of skepticism and trepidation. As inspirational as the city appeared to be for architects, visual artists, and aristocratic aesthetes in the early 20th century, a different view of the city emerged from modernist fiction. F. Scott Fitzgerald, John Dos Passos, and Thomas Wolfe all wrote city novels that questioned the frenetic pace of modern life and its various effects on the humanity that seemed to be getting left behind in the rush toward . . . well, no one really knew toward what. Progress for the sake of progress seemed to be the driving motive of modernity. In some ways, the creators of early superhero comic books also belong on the list of writers I just noted. Superhero comic books are often discussed only in connection with pulp fiction and film; critical conversations about the origins of the superhero genre rarely take into account media outside of 1930s popular culture. In fact, the image of the city that emerged from early superhero comic books matches up quite well with the literary trends that emerged from "traditional" fiction prior to and during the creation of comics. While not as verbally eloquent as the novels most scholars consider high art, early superhero books are in some ways just as complex, timely, and relevant in their portrayal of urban life as their more revered literary predecessors.

---

* The Civil War, which ended in 1865, effectively ended the agrarian economic structure of the South. It also led to a short-lived exodus of African Americans, both westward and northward, to Pittsburgh, Chicago, Cleveland, and New York City. (The next Great Migration of African Americans was in 1915, when many industrial jobs opened in the North after World War I began.) The first transcontinental railway, completed in 1869, would soon change the face of America both literally and figuratively. The period between the Civil War and World War I was one of massive immigration, largely from Germany, Ireland, and Poland. The growth of the cities was further expedited by technological innovations in productivity (Ford's assembly line), communication (telegraph and telephone), and transportation (the train and the car).

The experience of urban life—at least as expressed in art—was influenced not just by sociological and technological developments, but by philosophical developments as well. One important change modernism brought to art was a different approach to the concept of time. In his 1903 book *An Introduction to Metaphysics*, French philosopher Henri Bergson suggested that the human mind perceives real life not as a series of clearly marked conscious states, progressing along some imaginary line, but rather as a continuous flow. Whereas most people assumed (and still assume) that time is mechanical and orderly, Bergson argued that time is actually presented to consciousness as *duration*—an endlessly flowing process. Many scholars credit Bergson with the development of the theory of psychological relativity. Time didn't have to mean what it once did. The possibility of flexible temporal experience was exciting and heavily influential to many writers and artists of the modern age, especially in the development of stream-of-consciousness narrative. But to most ordinary Americans, Bergson's theories were meaningless. Subjective duration doesn't change the real-life demands of a 12- or 16-hour workday, any more than it changes the feeling of paralysis in a life that is literally passing by more quickly every day. In the face of modern mechanical speed, many Americans had to have felt immobilized by—unable to *catch* up with, much less *keep* up with—the pace of contemporary life. Speed was one of the major anxieties comic book superheroes were reacting to when they first debuted.

In modernist fiction, speed is most commonly represented by transportation, especially trains and automobiles. The rush of cars in the streets and the rattle of overhead and underground trains saturate city novels. Jay Gatsby is partially identified by his car, with which he glides into and out of New York City. Characters in the novel *Manhattan Transfer*, such as Bud Korpenning, constantly hear clacking from overhead and look up only in enough time to see the elevated train rushing around the next bend. At a time when basic human functions—labor, manual production, even running and walking—were becoming redundant and obsolete, superheroes were a refreshing assertion of organic, physical accomplishment. Superman was faster than a speeding bullet and taunted train conductors who gasped when they saw him speed by.* The Flash didn't walk and didn't even run in the way we think of running. He blew past cars and trains, and he raced up to the tops of buildings in less time than it took someone to fall from one. Here were characters capable of not only keeping up with but transcending the pace of modern life. If the protagonists of modernist novels were intimidated and paralyzed by modernity and lulled into a state of passivity, superheroes actively attempted to meet modernity head-on and race past it.

The forces of the city weren't just quick, though. They were also intimidating and powerful. Skyscrapers hovered overhead, blocking out the sun and dwarfing people who looked up and tried to comprehend them. By 1913, New York City had an imposing, substantial skyline that could boast over 200 floors of steel-skeleton construction.

---

* Each of the opening whole-page comic panels from the Superman stories in the early years of *Action Comics* demonstrated Superman performing some act of domination over some technological aspect of modern life (lifting cars and tanks, soaring above skyscrapers, etc.). *Action Comics* #14 (July 1939) shows Superman outrunning a locomotive.

In one of the New York chapters of *You Can't Go Home Again*, Thomas Wolfe subverts the apparent progress of the Manhattan skyscrapers by presenting a news story about a man who jumped from the top of one of them and splattered his brains across the concrete below. Wolfe's descriptions of the concrete jungle are impressive throughout the novel, but his characterization of the skyscraper suicide is particularly striking: "The pavement finally halts all, stops all, answers all. It is the American pavement, our universal city sidewalk, a wide, hard stripe of grey-white cement, blocked accurately with dividing lines. It is the hardest, coldest, cruelest, most impersonal pavement in the world: all of the indifference, the atomic desolation, the exploded nothingness of one hundred million nameless [men] is in it."[3] Trains, another symbol of the new industrial power, barreled between, through, over, and under cities with little regard for anyone who got in their path. In *Manhattan Transfer*, the elevated train rattles over the heads of characters like the cackle of mechanical gods. In an early chapter, a train runs into a carriage carrying a milkman named Gus McNiel, whose personal devastation unfolds in the remainder of the novel.

Whereas the power of the cities often overwhelms the protagonists of traditional modernist novels, the power of uncontrollable modern forces was counteracted by the strength of superhero protagonists. Although trains and automobiles are recognized as powerful and dangerous, the superhero is able to control, destroy, or redirect these energies more often than not. In what is probably the most iconic single image of Superman, the cover of *Action Comics* #1, the hero hoists a car above his head. He also power cleans train engines. He isn't dwarfed by skyscrapers but leaps over them in a single bound. The other heroes from these early years set a precedent for being able to do the same thing, even if their Bat-ropes were connected to no discernable anchor. (What's higher than a skyscraper?) Batman, Starman, and Green Lantern were all rendered soaring high above the lights and buildings of nighttime cityscapes. These characters seemed to be able to control the cities that threatened to assert control over everyone else.

As dangerous as cars and trains were to ordinary city denizens, the perceived threat from one another was far greater. As America shifted from an agrarian to an urban economy at the turn of the century, more and more people began living closer and closer together. These weren't people from the same places and classes who knew and trusted one another (or even spoke the same languages). Mines and factories brought many poorer citizens and immigrants to cities like New York, Chicago, and Pittsburgh near the end of the 19th century, and the demand for labor during the years of World War I brought even more people to major urban centers looking to make new beginnings. But many of these migrants discovered that the cities didn't always deliver on their promise. High unemployment, combined with Prohibition, which began in 1919 and lasted into the 1930s, created conditions ripe for the emergence of widespread organized crime. The Stock Market Crash of 1929 only exacerbated an already dismal situation. One consequence of all this was that, during the Depression years, urban dwellers began fearing poverty and crime—and ultimately each other— more than they ever had before. The crime-fighting that the superheroes engaged in during their formative years was borne of an immediate, direct concern over rising crime rates and social transition.

In fiction, John Dos Passos, Theodore Dreiser, and eventually John Steinbeck all used class and socioeconomic disparity to expose the human consequences of social inequity. At the end of *You Can't Go Home Again*, George Webber vows to correct the problems he has found in contemporary urban life: "Man's life can be, and will be, better;...man's greatest enemies, in the forms in which they now exist—the forms we see on every hand of fear, hatred, slavery, cruelty, poverty, and need—can be conquered and destroyed. But to conquer and destroy them will mean nothing less than the complete revision of the structure of society as we know it" (pp. 572–573). Although some American modernist novels of the 1920s and 1930s presented a hesitant hope that man could contend with life in the modern world, few offered evidence or long-term concrete solutions. Superhero comics countered passiveness and chaos by demonstrating characters beating back the forces of modernity. Every Superman story published in the first few years of *Action Comics* began with a narrative panel that in some ways echoed George Webber's sentiments in Wolfe's novel. *Action Comics* #16 begins with the following pronouncement: "Friend of the helpless and oppressed is Superman, a man possessing the strength of a dozen Samsons! Lifting and rending gigantic weights, vaulting over skyscrapers, racing a bullet, possessing a skin impenetrable to even steel, are his physical assets used in this one-man battle against evil and injustice!" This passage is not as poetic as Wolfe's, certainly, but it does actively confront the issues George Webber seeks to correct.

The difficulties of modernity were by no means confined to the external world. As important as cities were to the development of modern art, literature, and their merger (comics), the internal landscape of the mind was just as important. In his notes, F. Scott Fitzgerald wrote, "Show me a hero and I will write you a tragedy."[4] Heroes—especially superheroes—are not supposed to be tragic. They are supposed to prevail against threat and danger. They are supposed to resist evil and temptation. They are supposed to be above reproach. But Fitzgerald's statement suggests that the hero in the modern world had become something quite different. The modernist hero is a pale reflection of classical heroism because he is an inherently flawed, imperfect product of an imperfect world. All of the great American modernist heroes—those immediately preceding comic book superheroes—are tragic characters, each with a prominent tragic flaw. Jay Gatsby is corrupt and terribly naïve; Frederic Henry is a war deserter; Thomas Sutpen is prideful and arrogant; even Tom Joad, perhaps the most classically heroic of the modernist American protagonists, spent a period of his life in jail for murder and can't seem to find a way to keep his family together.[*]

Confronting the depravity and growing worldwide sense of crisis in the 1930s was enough to lead many authors—as well as the protagonists of their fiction—toward pessimism and nihilism. Many of the most familiar characters from American modernism are consumed by the darker forces at work in the modern world (and, more

---

[*] Frederic Henry is from Ernest Hemingway's *A Farewell to Arms* (1929). Thomas Sutpen is from William Faulkner's *Absalom, Absalom!* (1936). Tom Joad is from John Steinbeck's *The Grapes of Wrath* (1939).

important, by their personal inadequate response to their world). The superhero comic book, replete with mad scientists, crooks, and murderers, also accepts the fallen state and difficulties of the modern world. If a form of despair emerged from those early stories, it was the same sense of despair that emerged from modernist literature as a whole—a fear that the modern world was moving too quickly and that too many fundamental parts of humanity were being lost in the process. The superhero was intended to provide a remedy for this fear. The early comic book creators accepted the type of world that had been presented in modernist novels. The modern world was an overwhelming place, one of doubt and uncertainty, chaos and disorder. But rather than allow their characters to fall into the wells of despair and yield to the temptations of corruption that had enticed the protagonists of many modernist novels, the superhero creators tried to forge characters who could transcend the limitations of contemporary existence and stave off the chaos of the modern world. Superman creators Siegel and Shuster, Batman co-creator Kane, and the others reflected many of the anxieties of urban life, but it was the superhero who could keep these social disturbances in check. The superheroes of the 1930s and 1940s could not be broken easily. They could be bound, cut, pounded, burned, or weakened by exposure to green rocks, but they never really lost.

In 1905, Henry Adams closed his autobiographical tome *The Education of Henry Adams* with this musing about himself and two of his friends:

> Education had ended for all three, and only beyond some remoter horizon could its values be fixed or renewed. Perhaps some day—say 1938, their centenary,—they might be allowed to return together for a holiday, to see the mistakes of their own lives made clear in the light of the mistakes of their successors; and perhaps then, for the first time since man began his education among the carnivores, they would find a world that sensitive and timid natures could regard without a shudder.[5]

Throughout *The Education*, Adams's reflections on the close of the 19th century and the dawning of the 20th are dark and contain many justifiable fears and anxieties about the years that would follow. The most interesting part of the book's closing passage, however, is the coincidental throwaway date Adams provides: 1938. This was, of course, the year in which Jerry Siegel and Joel Shuster created a genre that, while more simplistic and naïve than its fine-arts contemporaries, answered modernist apprehensions with action, assertiveness, positivity, and clarity (all attributes that would be applied to great effect during World War II). Superheroes were borne of modernity, but they were also a direct response to it. Superhero comics have always provided a mirror for American culture and society. In every decade, comics have reflected the principal concerns and transitions of modern life. As contemporary American mythology, superheroes are extraordinarily adaptable. But nearly everything that defines superheroes—from their costumes to their powers to their sense of purpose and mission—roots them firmly in the modernist age of the early 20th century.

NOTES

1. James Joll. *Three Intellectuals in Politics*. New York: Pantheon Books, 1960, pp. 179–184.

2. Bill Finger and Bob Kane. "Batman and Robin Visit the 1940 New York World's Fair." *New York World's Fair Comics*, 1940 issue. New York: DC Comics.

3. Thomas Wolfe. *You Can't Go Home Again*. New York: Harper & Row, 1973, p. 368. Wolfe's novel was originally published posthumously in 1940.

4. F. Scott Fitzgerald. *The Crack-Up*. New York: New Directions, 1970, p. 122.

5. Henry Adams. *The Education of Henry Adams*. Boston: Massachusetts Historical Society, 2007. *Education* was originally completed in 1907 and published in 1918.

SEVEN

Heroes of the Superculture

Richard Reynolds

A British citizen trained in English literature and Anglo-American studies, Richard Reynolds teaches and writes about comics and superheroes, among other topics. He is the author of the seminal book *Superheroes: A Modern Mythology*. Reynolds is working on his next book, *Superculture*, from which his essay below is drawn. A Senior Lecturer at Central Saint Martins College of Arts and Design in London, he has been reading and collecting superhero comics since 1978.

I was not the first anomaly to exist…but on that day of my freedom in 1939, this world had its first confrontation with the fantastic.
— The Human Torch (Kurt Busiek and Alex Ross, *Marvels 1*. New York: Marvel Comics, 1994)

Technology has the ability to extend not only human capability and experience, but also, crucially, the human *personality*. We inhabit a world where GPS, digital TV, the Internet, and the mobile phone have revolutionized everybody's lives. Through Facebook, Twitter, and other social media, everyone can now live their life as the protagonist of their own digital narrative. All of this now seems unremarkable, as does the ease with which we are able to adopt alter egos, avatars, and aliases through the Internet. But, in this brave new digital landscape, where are the myths to lend universality to our experience? Where are the heroes who will give visible dimension to our complex identities? They already exist, and have been waiting for decades for our society to catch up with them. The mythic heroes of our information age are the costumed superheroes. The superhero is a protagonist in the cycle of mythology that has evolved to express and mediate the expansion of human action and identity in the post-industrial age.

During the year of 1938, a remarkable and unprecedented new publication was unleashed on the unsuspecting American public. The work in question was both radical and bizarre in the concepts that it embraced, and so speculative in its attitude toward human potential and its global point of view that it reached print only after two years of doubt, hesitation, and double-checking by its eventual publisher. Publication would launch a popular American cultural hero on a unique trajectory. The impact of this individual is still with us today, completing (in the words of his own mission statement) the "experiment, to find what a single individual can contribute to changing the world and benefiting all humanity."*

The book in question is *Nine Chains to the Moon*, the first full-length publication by the architect, designer, and futurologist R. Buckminster Fuller.[1] The title itself perfectly expresses the radical realignment of our assumptions that Fuller achieves: the

---

* This remark is very widely attributed to Fuller, and admirably sums up his philosophy, but there does not seem to be a single authoritative source for the quotation.

nine chains refer to the total height that could be attained if all of the human beings alive in 1938 could have been induced to stand on each other's shoulders—a human measure, but interplanetary in its reach and scope. This metaphor is painstakingly expounded by Fuller in order to prepare the reader's imagination for his subsequent flights of speculative thinking, inviting us to reject established thought patterns and embrace the potential of the coming post-industrial age.

The year 1938 was particularly rich in dramatic events that seemed to presage the arrival of a new era. Many of these were military and political—the Russian show trials, the German–Austrian Anschluss and the occupation of the Sudetenland, and the formation in the U.S. Congress of the House Un-American Activities Committee. Even the sporting world seemed to mirror political struggles elsewhere. On June 22, heavyweight boxing champion Joe Louis knocked out the German challenger, and favorite of Adolf Hitler, Max Schmeling, in the first round of their rematch at New York City's Yankee Stadium. The coming war cast its shadow everywhere. On October 30, Orson Welles and his Mercury Theater famously sparked off a mass panic with their documentary-style radio adaptation of H. G. Wells's classic science fiction story *The War of the Worlds* and its tale of alien invasion. If we can reach up for the stars, the stars may also reach down for us. By November 1938, construction of the production plant for the V2 rocket had begun in Germany, at Peenemünde.

The late 1930s also saw an acceleration in the augmentation of the mind, body, and senses through the application of technology and design. This period can plausibly be said to mark the genesis of the information culture that we inhabit today. Other dramatic events seem to be prophecies of the technology-driven affluence that lay somewhere beyond the abyss of World War II. The new discoveries and marvels of 1938 included the following:

- The demonstration in London of the first Baird color television
- The marketing of the first mass-produced nylon products from Du Pont (toothbrushes)
- Hungarian inventor (and comics publisher) Lazlo Biro's invention of the ballpoint pen
- Swiss chemist Albert Hofmann's discovery of lysergic acid diethylamide-25 (otherwise known as LSD)
- German inventor Konrad Zuse's first programmable computer
- Howard Hughes's flight around the world in a new record of 3 days, 19 hours, and 14 minutes
- The discovery of oil in Kuwait
- American physicist Charles Critchfield's proposal of hydrogen fusion as a source of stellar energy
- British engineer G. S. Callendar's paper outlining the first scientific evidence of global warming[2]

In April 1938, an extraordinary new hero who seemed to embody and yet also surpass so many of these new marvels made his debut in the first issue of *Action*

Comics: Superman.* Jerry Siegel and Joe Shuster's new costumed hero—as is well documented—endured as troubled a journey into print as did Fuller's *Nine Chains to the Moon*. Just as Fuller was obliged to acquire the support and approval of Albert Einstein before his publisher truly believed in the project, Siegel and Shuster served an apprenticeship by creating the relatively conventional detective strip *Slam Bradley* before their publisher National Allied (the forerunner of DC Comics) became convinced that the world was ready for their masterpiece, the Man of Tomorrow.

The superhero narrative was the first (and arguably, so far, the only) new myth to express the expansion of human action and identity in the post-industrial age. In today's society, the effects of technological development have become ubiquitous, and its cultural products range from the instant celebrity of reality TV to the alternate universe of Second Life. But it is remarkable that such an enduring myth of the information age—the superhero—should have been created so early in the post-industrial era. Hindsight is easy, but it takes genius to craft a myth that will interpret the conflicts of an era that has barely begun. Yet, although the world of 1938 might now seem remote, the pressing issues of our contemporary world were already being sensed by advanced and innovative thinkers, as the list above illustrates. Computers, color TV, designer drugs, nuclear power, global warming—all of these threats and marvels were visible on the mental horizon of the late 1930s.

Given that he was born at the dawn of the information age, it is appropriate (as well as an excellent storytelling device) that Siegel and Shuster made Clark Kent a newspaper reporter. As early as *Superman* #4,[3] the narrative becomes concerned with issues that remain central to the information society—questions of intellectual property and licensing.† Kent is introduced by his editor (not yet known as Perry White) to a man named Williams, who asserts that he is "Superman's personal manager." Williams claims to be in possession of a contract giving him exclusive merchandising rights to Superman's name. Kent and his editor are skeptical, but the fast-talking Williams offers the *Daily Star* (as Kent's employer was known in the earliest stories) exclusive Superman press coverage. Williams rattles off a list of other licensing deals that he claims are already in place, including Superman bathing suits, costumes, physical development exercisers, and movie rights, and finishes by declaring, "Why, I've even made provisions for him to appear in the comics!"

Needless to say, Williams is a fraudster. The "Superman" he represents is an actor, supporting the deception with stage props and gimmicks. But before the inevitable exposure of the scheme, Williams has occasion, in conversation with his actor-stooge, to make a trenchant observation: "I figured that seeing as Superman is probably just a myth, someone might as well cash in on the publicity!" In other words, the myth of Superman had already become more important to the media

---

* *Action Comics* #1 is cover-dated for June but was published in April 1938 by National Allied Publications, a corporate predecessor of DC Comics.

† How ironic, given the subsequent struggles that Siegel and Shuster experienced in attempting to obtain the creator's rights to their own character.

than any of Superman's individual heroic actions. I find it remarkable to encounter, so early on, such ironic awareness by Siegel and Shuster of the true nature of the myth they had created.

Public perception can turn a hero into a villain overnight, as Superman and other superheroes have periodically learned to their cost. For the mutant superheroes of the X-Men, negative media and public perception are permanent afflictions. Superheroes are born into the information age. If they do not seize control of their media identity, they risk the loss of their heroic status.

Robin Hood, William Tell, Johnny Appleseed—these heroes operated in splendid isolation from the problems of celebrity and media scrutiny. Their legends are told in hindsight, not reinvented on the hoof through an interactive dialogue with their audience. The folk heroes of the early American West, such as Billy the Kid, William "Buffalo Bill" Cody, or Jesse James, inhabited a different world. Advances in communications and the growth of print media made the recording and re-telling of their exploits and their consequent fame a part of the myth itself. Cinema has repeatedly portrayed the Western hero as a protagonist intent on carving out his destiny in the autonomous manner of an earlier age, but circumscribed and, in many cases, ultimately destroyed by the very forces that disseminate his legend. These tragic Western heroes find it impossible to escape, even temporarily, from the consequences of their celebrity.

Superheroes have been adopting secret identities since *Action Comics* #1, but the superheroes themselves have seldom shrunk from publicity. Take, for example, the characterization of the original Stan Lee–Steve Ditko Spider-Man (*Amazing Spider-Man* #1–#38).[4] Spider-Man's alter ego Peter Parker bears more than a passing resemblance to Clark Kent: he works for a newspaper, he acts nerdy, and he is perennially unlucky in love. As a costumed hero operating outside the law, Spider-Man cannot automatically rely on the support of the authorities. His position depends on public opinion and the media. Spider-Man fights against many memorable costumed villains, but his archenemy is his employer at the *Daily Bugle*, the irascible J. Jonah Jameson, a man who is convinced that Spider-Man is a public menace. The battles between Spider-Man and his publisher are fought for the control of public opinion. Jameson is Spider-Man's most relentless superpowered antagonist. His superpower is information based: he has the power to decide what makes news.

The economic relationship between Parker and the *Daily Bugle* is acutely drawn. Parker supplements his income by selling pictures of Spider-Man to the *Bugle*—pictures that are easy for him to get, thanks to his secret-identity. But these photographs are used by Jameson only to further his hate campaign against Spider-Man. Parker is trapped in the uncomfortable position of contributing to the demonization of his alter ego every time he sells a Spider-Man photograph, feeding the legend that might destroy him. In *Amazing Spider-Man* #25, Jameson's media-based superpowers are extended into literal superpowers when an inventor named Smythe visits the offices of the *Bugle*. Smythe has perfected a remote-controlled, steel-tentacled robot capable of subduing Spider-Man, and he tries to interest Jameson in giving it a trial. Jameson dismisses Smythe as a crackpot. It takes all Parker's powers of persuasion to convince Jameson to give the invention a trial, Parker's motive being to obtain exclusive photographs of the encounter with Spider-Man.

Operating the robot from the safety of his newspaper office and seeing as well as being seen from a TV screen on the front of the bizarre device, Jameson tracks down Spider-Man and attacks him with this formidable invention. Spider-Man is fortunate to survive the encounter. An aggressive and intrusive steel octopus with a television screen for a face—has there been a sharper metaphor for the invasive character of the news media? Jameson's robot symbolizes a darker side of the expansion of human capabilities first celebrated by Siegel and Shuster.

During the first decade of the 21st century, the superhero movie became the most successful genre product in Hollywood. There may be several explanations for this. In the past decade, the studios have finally treated superheroes seriously and have developed scripts that deal in three-dimensional characters and stories with a resonance that can engage the wider public (*Dark Knight*, *Iron Man*, the second *Hulk* movie, *Kick-Ass*).* But this is not the whole story. Something in the superhero myth has come of age. The concerns of the superhero genre have become the concerns of the moviegoing public.

The term *global superculture* was first coined by the economist Kenneth Boulding in 1969.[5] The phrase has subsequently been used to describe both the global information society first identified by Marshall McLuhan and the privileged lives of billionaires and their associates that this global village supports and facilitates. The term has developed as an antithesis to the term *subculture*, which refers to a group of people marginalized from the cultural mainstream. Members of a superculture choose to hide from public view in order to protect themselves. Movie stars go on shopping trips wearing dark glasses, hoods, and headscarves. The super-rich and super-famous congregate in locations inaccessible to the average citizen and are cautious about flaunting their wealth and celebrity elsewhere. The superculture exists in a sphere removed from everyday life and becomes vulnerable if displaced. By travelling incognito, members of the superculture adopt one of the key traits of the superhero. Some off-duty superheroes, it could be added, have always inhabited this billionaire superculture: Reed Richards, Tony Stark, Bruce Wayne, Adrian Veidt. They live both sides of their lives far removed from the experience of their fellow human beings.

Superheroes have the rare ability to communicate outside their narrative context. Some have entered the fabric of popular culture at the very deepest level, and their mythology is used to elucidate many facets of everyday life—even by those who might never read a superhero comic or watch a superhero film. The superhero myth anticipated global superculture in many ways. Both are deeply concerned with issues

---

* *The Incredible Hulk* (2008), *Iron Man* (2008), *Iron Man 2* (2010), *The Dark Knight* (2008), *Kick-Ass* (2010). What a shame that it isn't appropriate to mention the plodding film adaptation of *Watchmen* (2009) in this list of recent Hollywood creative successes.

of identity and the effective use of hidden power. By having anticipated several key aspects of the era in which we live, the superhero mythology can sometimes appear to comprehend the underlying or implicit nature of our contemporary world, reducing its tensions and conflicts to specific images and temporarily bringing irreducibly complex issues within the domain of narrative logic. This process might underscore the new success of the superhero movie.

Perhaps the time is now ripe to coin a new term: *Superculture* (with a capital "S"). This Superculture could be understood to refer not only to the collective text of narratives and mythology first created during the Golden Age of superhero comics, and subsequently sustained through to the present day, but also the presence of the superhero myth in television, movies, and other merchandising. Comic book Superculture—an avant-garde product of the 1930s—has been continually extrapolated, refined, and developed up to our present day. Once upon a time Jimmy Olsen had a special watch that he could use to talk to his friend Superman. Now everybody has a cell phone (and young people don't wear watches). The expansion of human action and the acquisition of multiple identities are no longer solely the prerogative of superheroes and their associates. Anti-virus software fights malicious malware, like a digital hero ceaselessly battling our hidden enemies in cyberspace. The concepts of "transhumanity" and "post-humanity" have now entered the social mainstream.* Within the Superculture, humanity exists in a state of imminent self-transcendence, in which science, technology, mind-and-body management, mythology, magic, and happenstance all play a role. The limits of the possible exist to be surpassed, whether by accident (the Flash, the Fantastic Four), design (Batman, Iron Man), or a combination of these (Daredevil, Rorschach, Wolverine).

If superhero mythology justly celebrates the successful expansion of human potential, why do we not now live in a post-industrial utopia? Why do citizens of the developed world work longer hours and experience greater stress than in earlier decades? Why do they live in fear of crime, terrorism, and unemployment? What has gone wrong with the great modernist enterprise? Having first appeared as avatars of the Western World's escape from the Great Depression and victory over fascism in World War II, superheroes are now required—after more than 75 years on the job—to explain why their presence in the world has not brought about a rational utopia. Is there a conspiracy that holds humanity back—as might be perpetrated by a supervillain such as Lex Luthor—or do our problems stem rather from our concept of what a hero should be? This theme has become central to many of the most intelligent superhero stories of the past 25 years.

Just as the intelligentsia of the 1930s faced the Great Depression, the rise of fascism, and the failure of technology to provide answers to economic and social problems, so contemporary superhero narratives are engaged in examining the limitations and failures of the Superculture that the genre announced and embodied. The genre's self-reflexive questioning has become a central concern.

---

* Transhumanism as a philosophical movement may be defined as the deliberate extension of human capacity through the use of science and technology. Posthumanism can be defined as the as-yet-unrealized outcome of this process.

In pioneering graphic novels such as Frank Miller's *Batman: The Dark Knight Returns* and Alan Moore's *Watchmen*, there is a direct and often satirical focus on the inability of the superhero to address the underlying causes of society's ills. Without supervillains to oppose them, the superpowered characters in *Watchmen* become political pawns and can even be driven—as in the case of Ozymandias—to fabricate a fake menace in order to achieve their own messianic ends. *The Dark Knight* (both the film and the graphic novel) is another superhero narrative in which society's collective support is withdrawn from the lone vigilante, who fights not only against crime but also against the social, political, and even spiritual malaise that makes violent crime inevitable.

The numerical growth of superpowered characters and the social consequences of this proliferation have also become key motifs. Chris Claremont's *X-Men* initiated the exploration of this theme back in the 1970s.* The problems experienced by a society of superpowered beings (as portrayed in *Kingdom Come*, *Astro City*, or *Top Ten*) implicitly comment on a world in which every citizen has the power to augment his or her own identity and personality through the power of technology.

What is a superhero today? Peter Coogan's three attributes of mission, powers, and identity[6] remain the most precise and concise definition. But the superhero's extended powers and complex identity now mirror more than ever the era in which we live. Ordinary people now have superpowers. The gifts of digital technology have enabled millions to experience their own "confrontations with the fantastic." Average human beings may now engage with the consequences of creating multiple identities and encircle the planet—if they wish to—with their virtual presence. Celebrities and members of the global superculture enact these same processes at an even higher level of power and visibility. Within this celebrity- and communications-obsessed culture, the superhero can now be seen as the key protagonist in a vast cycle of mythology that has evolved to express and mediate this unprecedented expansion of human action and identity.

NOTES

1. R. Buckminster Fuller, *Nine Chains to the Moon*, First Edition. Philadelphia: J.B. Lippincott, 1938. Page references here are to the paperback edition, published by Anchor in 1971.
2. G. S. Callendar. (1938). "The Artificial Production of Carbon Dioxide and Its Influence on Climate." *Quarterly Journal of the Royal Meteorological Society*, 64, pp. 223–240.
3. National Allied Publications, Spring 1940.
4. New York: Marvel Comics, March 1963–June 1966. Spider-Man fi rst appeared in *Amazing Fantasy* #15 (August 1962).
5. Kenneth E. Boulding. (1969). "The Interplay of Technology and Values: The Emerging Superculture." In J. Baier and N. Rescher (Eds.), *Values and the Future*. New York: Free Press, 1969.
6. Peter Coogan. (2006). *Superhero: The Secret Origin of a Genre*. Austin, TX: Monkeybrain Books, pp. 30–33.

* Subsequent stories to address this theme include Steve Englehart's *Green Lantern Corps*, *Astro City*, and *Kingdom Come*; Alan Moore's *Top Ten*; Geoff Johns' *Green Lantern Corps*; Brian Michael Bendis' *House of M* and many more.

EIGHT

Superheroes by Design

John Jennings

John Jennings holds an MFA in art and design with a concentration in graphic design and is both a comic book professional and a scholar. He is a comic book illustrator (and has designed superhero and other comic book characters), as well as co-author of the graphic novel *The Hole: Consumer Culture* (Volume 1) and co-editor and designer of *Black Comix: African American Independent Comics, Art and Culture*. He curates art exhibitions of the comics medium and teaches various courses related to design.

There are few visual symbols that communicate as effectively and with such consistency as the American pop-culture invention of the superhero. Indeed, it would be difficult to find someone in modern society who has never been exposed to the idea or representation of a superhero or the conventions of the genre. In my opinion, a superhero is one of the most effective visual communication vehicles ever designed.

Building on the fact that the superhero is a visual artifact, it is my aim to point out several formal qualities that help to solidify some of the reasons that superheroes resonate with us so intensely. The visual signifiers of symmetry, design, the reified body, costume, and color symbolism play vital roles in distinguishing characters who are superheroes from characters who aren't. Although the meaning of the superhero has been discussed for many years in various contexts, we must not forget that the superhero is first and foremost shorthand for conveying particular meanings in a visual mode.

SUPER IDEAS/SUPER BODIES

The superhero is a symbol of power that is reified as the hyper-physical body, and that body then comes to be a visual representation of that power. In *Practices of Looking* by Marita Sturken and Lisa Cartwright, *reification* is defined as the "process by which abstract ideas are rendered concrete. This means that material objects, such as commodities are awarded the characteristics of human subjects."[1]

The perfect body of the superhero is an object of cultural production that stands for many socially constructed ideas regarding power, justice, and morality. Possible antecedents of the superhero's body might be the beautiful sculptures of ancient Greece and Rome, which depicted beauty that was then thought to be classic and therefore perfect in mind and spirit. In a sense, the superhero is exactly that, an illustration of the perfect fusion of mind, body, and spirit. The superhero body performs and displays these reified ideas to a public that still values these basic tenets today. The superhero is an embodiment, but not just of an individual. It is an embodiment of cultural and social values—a *gestalt* of various belief structures in physical form.

In addition to being a metaphorical body, the superhero body is one seen in motion. It leaps, crushes, crouches, pounces, and flies. Superheroes are meant to be virtuous, selfless, brave, strong, and honorable. These qualities of the hero are displayed, acted, and explicitly executed. To match the ideas and beliefs that motivate the superheroes' behaviors, the body must be shown to be powerful and perfect.

The most prominent superheroes use their muscles and their minds in tandem to achieve their goal of saving the day. These qualities are laid out very successfully by Peter Coogan in *Superhero: The Secret Origin of a Genre*.[2] Coogan states that superheroes can be identified by a selfless mission, powers, and a distinct identity composed of a code name and an iconic costume. If you look at the three tenets of mind, body, and spirit, they align quite nicely with Coogan's categories. A focused mind relates to mission. The mind's thoughts spark the beginnings of the superhero's mission. The body—reified power—relates very closely to superheroes' physical display of might. Lastly, the idea of a living spirit can also relate to the individual *essence* or *soul*. Therefore, spirit can possibly be equated with identity. I imagine this trinity to be in the shape of an equilateral triangle. The triangle is a testament to the idea of the divine body and an example of how symmetry plays an important part in superheroes and their formally communicative properties.

SUPER SYMMETRY

The principle of *symmetry* can be found everywhere in nature. It is part of our environment and our very bodies. In addition to this ubiquity, it can affect our very notions of what we deem important. Symmetry comes in various forms. It is a perceived notion of balance and harmony. Bilateral symmetry, in which the two sides of a form are mirrored, is very common in all forms of life. In *Making Comics*, Scott McCloud[3] refers to this visual principle and its importance in his chapter on basic character design. He states, "Symmetry is life's calling card, the way we've learned to recognize each other in the wild. It's that bit of ourselves that breeds affection when we see it in our nearer relatives (simians) and makes us uneasy when we see it in our more distant ones (insects). It's the key ingredient that says 'Yes, this is an animal like me. This is a living thing.'"[4] Bilateral symmetry is useful for conveying information because the brain tends to remember it more clearly. McCloud states that in fact, "no matter how abstract or stylized a piece of art is, if it displays that basic arrangement, humans will see themselves in its features."[5]

In nature, certain animals take symmetry into account when choosing a mate. The female house sparrow uses the relative symmetry and size of the male's black bill in choosing a mating partner.[6] Symmetry is an important component of displays of strength and fitness in the Japanese scorpionfly when it competes for food to give as tribute to potential mates.[7] Also, a male blue peacock's chance of mating with a female is based on the number of eyespots, or *occelli*, coupled with the relative perception of symmetry attributed to the occelli paterns.[8] Symmetry is beautiful and desirable. Individuals we humans consider to be beautiful or attractive are likely to have faces and bodies we perceive as symmetrical. This, of course, suggests that people we think of as attractive would receive more attention from potential sexual partners and more opportunities to mate. It is also important to note that the various forms of life on our planet aren't actually bilaterally symmetrical, and that perfect bilateral symmetry is *perceived* and therefore contextual. In fact, if life forms were perfectly symmetrical, the resulting images would look odd and artificial. Therefore, this perfect symmetry isn't actually attainable physically, but it is very much desired.

For a discussion of superheroes, it is important to consider symmetry because it is a primary property of the chevron designs of the most memorable and lasting superhero characters.* Batman, Wonder Woman, Spider-Man, the Silver Age Green Lantern,[†] the X-Men, Iron Man, Captain America, Captain Marvel (from Marvel Comics), and many others use symmetry in their iconic symbols. Even Superman's "S," though asymmetrical in design, is presented within a symmetrical diamond shape. This simple and elegant design strategy is a key element in a strong formal presentation of the superhero body and its implied connotations of balance, justice, goodness, strength, power, and perfection. Symmetry, both physical and metaphorical, is the language of the superhero in various ways.

It is also the language of various cosmologies and belief structures. Scott McCloud states in *Understanding Comics* that "symbols are the stuff from which gods are made."[9] It is fascinating that the connections among superheroes, ancient mythology, and religion are inferred by comics scholars and fans alike. Bilateral symmetry is a major component of religious and metaphysical iconography. The Christian cross, the Christian fish symbol, the Jewish Star of David, the *veves* used in Haitian Voudou,[‡] Buddhist mandalas, the infinity symbol, and the Egyptian *ankh* all employ this type of imagery. Perhaps the term "hero worship" isn't too far-fetched in this context? Superheroes are our modern messiahs, and they can represent clarity of vision, heroism, balance, sacrifice, and rebirth. These are qualities that people have valued both in our contemporary society and throughout human history.

Even the superheroes of the decidedly deconstructionist *Watchmen*, by Alan Moore and Dave Gibbons, employ various levels of symmetry to show the interlocking concepts of chaos and order.[10] The Comedian's "smiley face" button, Rorschach's heat-sensitive mask, and Doctor Manhattan's forehead chevron all use symmetry in their designs. Those symmetrical visual aspects, plus the nature of these superheroes' histories and personal relationships, make these three the most memorable characters in the graphic novel.

In addition, the classic "Superman pose" reifies these ideas about symmetry and "goodness." We have all seen this pose performed and sometimes lampooned. The feet are far apart. The body is facing forward in order to maximize the physical nature

---

* Editors' note: *Chevron* is comic book artist Jim Steranko's term for the superhero chest symbol or insignia, such as Superman's "S" shield, Batman's bat, Spider-Man's spider, or the Fantastic Four's "F." Peter Coogan popularized the use of *chevron* in *Superhero: The Secret Origin of the Superhero*.

† Editors' note: The Green Lantern of the Silver Age generally refers to the character of Hal Jordan from the 1950s and 1960s.

‡ *Veves* are the written symbols used during ceremonies in the religion of Voudou (Voodoo). Each veve corresponds to a particular god or spirit (loa) and is used to call that particular spirit to ask its aid or blessing.

of the pose. The chest is lifted high to show the symmetrical chevron as clearly as possible. The fists are placed on the hips with the elbows locked at a 90-degree angle. This stance can be read as an amplified *performance* of symmetry and all it implies. Scott McCloud references this type of body language in *Making Comics*. He states, "A ramrod straight posture, like the one seen in a lot of superhero books, will communicate strength and confidence by being symbolically taller."[11] The image of McCloud's avatar demonstrates the pose with the labels "chin up," "chest out," and "back arched" as performance signifiers. He goes on to state that asymmetry can connote various negative emotional traits and that this principle can be used by comics creators to create tension and display conflicts of various kinds.

Well-thought-out costume design can help magnify this performance. The amplification of visually symmetrical qualities is evident in details of certain superhero costume designs such as Wolverine's mask, the winged helmet of the mighty Thor, Doctor Strange's huge collar, and Batman's pointy ears on the side of his cowl. These are deliberate displays of symmetry and power that are reminiscent of the aforementioned blue peacock and his self-conscious strutting for attention.

COSTUMES AND COLOR SYMBOLISM

Superheroes wear costumes. The costume is the most recognizable visual aspect of the genre and of the characters. The rationales for these costumes are as varied as the characters themselves. The skintight costume seems directly connected to the display, performance, and execution of the reified connotations of the culture that are represented by the perfect physique of the superhero. Those bodies must be seen. The skintight costume is a medium for displaying the superhero's physicality. This visual convention has significantly affected the depiction of these characters for decades. In *The Power of Comics*, Randy Duncan and Matthew J. Smith state, "In the 1960s artists like Neal Adams and Jim Steranko revived (Burne) Hogarth's flayed look, in which every muscle stands in sharp relief, as if the covering skin had been removed."[12] They go on to state that "because comics are a visual medium, the ritualistic display of a hero's power has become another stylistic convention of the superhero genre."[13]

Another component of the costume is, of course, color. Superhero costumes tend toward the primary colors of red, yellow, and blue (and, conversely, supervillain costumes tend toward the secondary colors of orange, green, and purple, though these tendencies are by no means absolute or universal). Many historians, including Scott McCloud, attribute this color preference to the need of comics creators to differentiate their protagonists from the rest of the characters. McCloud states in *Understanding Comics*, "These colors objectify their subjects. We become more aware of the physical form of objects than in black and white."[14] Duncan and Smith echo this observation by saying that "the connection between color and superheroes is so prominent that some creators working in other genres have consciously avoided the use of color, choosing to work in black and white in order to distance themselves from the (potentially) juvenile connotation of bright color."[15] A connection between particular colors with bright tonal ranges and the superhero genre can be made in certain contexts.

In summation, the superhero is a compelling visual communication vehicle that utilizes tried and true design elements coupled with powerful social connotations in order to convey specific ideologies connected to our society's beliefs and cultural practices. The visual signifiers of the superhero resonate with us—the physical performance of the powers, the superhero costume (which highlights the design element of color and the principle of symmetry), and the display of the physically fit body. We sense the inherent combination of these qualities and respond accordingly. As a result, the visual cues of the superhero are learned, processed, and disseminated in our culture and transmitted as modern mythology via various media. The superhero is a classic American visual convention that has stood the test of time. The form persists today because of great conceptual design and application by generations of comics creators. Superheroes represent what we want to be, either physically or spiritually. As long as there is evil to conquer and injustices to make right, the superhero will be there to symbolize the struggles we all must endure in our personal journeys to vanquish the foes within ourselves.

NOTES

1. Lisa Cartwright and Marita Sturken. (2001). *Practices of Looking: An Introduction to Visual Culture*. New York: Oxford University Press, p. 364.
2. Peter Coogan. (2006). *Superhero: The Secret Origin of a Genre*. Austin, TX: MonkeyBrain Books.
3. Scott McCloud. (2006). *Making Comics: Storytelling Secrets of Comics, Manga and Graphic Novels* New York: HarperCollins.
4. McCloud, *Making*, p. 59.
5. McCloud, *Making*, p. 60.
6. Jeffry B. Mitton. (2000). *Selection in Natural Populations* New York: Oxford University Press, p. 136.
7. Mitton, *Selection*, p. 136.
8. Mitton, *Selection*, p. 136.
9. Scott McCloud. (1993). *Understanding Comics: The Invisible Art* Northampton, MA: Kitchen Sink Press/Harper Perennial, p. 188.
10. Alan Moore and David Gibbons, *Watchmen*. New York: DC Comics, 1986.
11. McCloud, *Making*, p. 106.
12. Randy Duncan and Matthew J. Smith. (2009). *The Power of Comics: History, Form, and Culture*. New York: Continuum Press, p. 235.
13. Duncan and Smith, *Power of Comics,* p. 236.
14. McCloud, *Understanding*, p. 189.
15. Duncan and Smith, *Power of Comics,* p. 236.

NINE

The Experience of the Superhero: A Phenomenological Definition

Dana Anderson

Dana Anderson earned his PhD in English and has also studied phenomenological philosophy. Although he's written for many years about visual arts, this is his first time writing about superheroes and the world in which they arise.

The ultimate motto of phenomenology is, "To the things themselves!" Thus, in order to understand what the superhero is, a phenomenologist has to return to the experience of that particular thing. However, "superhero" is a generalization, a term created to define a set of imaginary beings; it is an abstraction that distills from the set of all unique superheroes certain key characteristics. As such, the superhero is not a substantial thing to which a phenomenologist can easily (or, more important, usefully) return. You might even say that it is not a thing at all (except insofar as it is a word).

Looking at the idea of the superhero from a phenomenological perspective means trying to find the visceral experience one has of "superheroness" in the world, perhaps by analyzing an encounter with a comics shop that sells only superhero books. In other words, one needs to find a concrete experience that manifests superheroness in order to analyze it phenomenologically. Unfortunately, in order to understand this kind of experience, one needs data from multiple discrete encounters. A collective experience as such is hard to find, and phenomenology is much more useful for examining specific things than abstractions. Because of this, I have chosen to leave definitions of the generality to other writers in this volume (which in a sense represents a collective vision of the superhero) and instead work from my own specific experiences of encounters with individual superheroes in my daily life.

It may seem that analyzing a specific encounter avoids the actual question, which requires a general answer. However, we need to keep in mind that collective experiences, like that of the superhero, are actually a sum of many individual encounters. Each superhero starts as an idea, is translated onto paper in drawings and words, and is then published. As the first issue or strip reaches out into the world, primary relationships are formed with readers. Over time, if the superhero is successful, a collective relationship begins to form between him or her and an audience that stretches across time. As readers experience him or her, this gestalt relationship begins to form around those encounters, generating a group dynamic through which the superhero evolves into an icon. The superhero needs a consistent audience, supported by a distribution system and enormous numbers of unique reading experiences, in order for this process to be possible. I think that one of the things that separate a superhero from an ordinary hero is the fact of this gestalt, group experience. Ordinary heroism is about single actions that reach out to a small group of people who are immediately affected by the heroic act. Perhaps a newspaper covers the heroism, and thus grants it an audience, or perhaps a film character acts heroically and is seen by many. These heroes might become role models, but their heroism is defined by the individual stories that made them important. With a superhero, you have no specific narrative that defines the relationship; the superhero will always act heroically, and because of this he or she falls out of time, becoming an expected part of the monthly life (in the case of a monthly comic) of a group of unique readers joined into a collective (the fans) by this ongoing experiential activity. Phenomenology gives us tools with which to analyze the individual elements of the collective experience of the system of interactions necessary for the becoming of a superhero, so that we can see them in their multilayered complexity.

The best way for me to demonstrate the use of these phenomenological tools is to write a small sample defining my own first encounter with "the superhero." As I go through the analysis of my own experience, each reader will ideally be able to take the phenomenological journey with me, and each person's reading of my essay will thus result in a paired (collective) definition of the term *superhero*. All the readings taken together (if they could be collated) would reach even deeper into the collective nature of the experience of the superhero. As I briefly discuss some aspects of my own encounters, each reader will, I hope, compare his or her story with mine, and new sets of patterns (very different ones than the others we're likely to see in this volume) will appear.

This phenomenological approach necessarily takes on what may be an unusual style, and that merits some explanation. Typically, academic writing comes in the form of an argument: it starts with a main idea (a thesis) that gets supported by other ideas, which end up proving the main point. Phenomenology starts instead with an experience, and there is no desire for a conclusion; rather, the exploration of the experience itself is the purpose of the writing, a non-predetermined intellectual journey through moments of being-in-the-world. In the end, points are made, but they will have arisen out of events that are related to the reader in what seems like autobiography.

Unlike other disciplines that have an ideology or interpretive point of view or particular jargon as their defining criteria, phenomenology is a pattern of looking at experience, beginning with a recognition that the experiencer's situation creates biases that are at the heart of his or her way of understanding and defining the world. To share my history with superheroes, I have chosen moments that bring out these biases, making my subject position very clear. I have also chosen moments that set the stage for the experience, giving it a context in time and space, and others that turned out to be keys to an understanding of the particulars of the superhero experience as I have lived it. This evocation of lived understanding is interrupted by moments of clarification in which the experience is broken down and results are discovered. This is the basic pattern of phenomenology.

My hope is that as you read, you'll follow my narrative with one of your own, and that you will find that my results lead to results of your own; thus, together, we will arrive, through our individual analyses, at a general definition of the experience of the superhero. In this way, my essay should help you read the others in this book with a more complete sense of your own perspective that will ideally make the experience of the book rounder and more complete.

When I was a little boy, in the early 1970s, my favorite superheroes were Dr. Strange and Captain Marvel (the Marvel version, not Shazam).* Their comics were deep experiences for me, unlike anything else I had ever read, because the word–image combination fired my head into a different kind of imaginary world, one that had no real beginning or conceivable end. It seemed that there would always be a new issue on its way to the spinner rack in the local store (an actual soda shop straight out of the early 20th century) where I went with my allowance money (a not irrelevant detail: my buying the comics meant they were mine in a way few things in my life were at that time, and if the books were mine, so were the dreams they gave me).

When I came home from that soda shop with my new comics, they held an incipient magic that it brings tears to my eyes to remember. I'd look at the covers for ages before opening them, and Dr. Strange and Captain Marvel would appear in my mind, not as characters from a book or a movie, but as reiterations of people I knew and respected and, more than anything else, wanted to be. At that point in my life (between the ages of 5 and 10), these people had also become part of my playscape, so they were part of my consciousness. Before going to sleep, I would imagine myself as one or the other of them and would take part in all kinds of new adventures. In looking at those covers, I was replaying not just the comics from the past year or so but all my dreams and games from the month since I had last held a new issue in my hands. The comics themselves weren't books so much as visits with friends who were also my dream selves and mentors for my future becoming.

When I opened the comics and the stories came to life before my eyes, they added information to the network of relationships that I had developed alongside them over the months of reading, dreaming, and playing. Even the style of the advertising took part in creating the shape of that reiterative experience. I'd be in the midst of a cosmic battle and, on the ad page, a group of Sea-Monkeys would beckon to me, or I'd encounter x-ray glasses and hover cars I could build in my spare time.† Everything was about the experience of being more than I could be in my little body, yet at the same time about being the best of what I already was. Dr. Strange and Captain Marvel were *my* heroes. They had a mystic consciousness that I shared, and a love of knowledge

---

* Dr. Strange was the Master of the Mystic Arts of the Marvel Universe. A former surgeon and scientist whose hands were injured in an auto accident, Dr. Strange found a new life studying wizardry with the Ancient One, a sorcerer of unparalleled wisdom. Captain Marvel was a Kree Warrior (from an alien empire far from Earth). He was charged with the task of observing Earth and became one of its greatest defenders. He had the ability to fly throughout the cosmos, super strength, and the power of cosmic awareness (an ability to become one with the universe). These characters were my alter egos at that time, my dream selves.

† Editors' note: Comic books have advertisements; frequently seen ads from the 1970s were for Sea-Monkeys (brine shrimp), x-ray glasses, and hover cars.

and science that I shared; then, on the other hand, their greatness filled gaps in me, filled the frightened spaces with hope and dreams not so much of glory as of empowered becoming. The ads would then provide a level of extra reality (the toys seemed to promise powers of their own: super strength, x-ray vision, flying, etc.), and Stan Lee would get on his soapbox, and I would listen, becoming part of a culture of people with similar dreams.* Then, when I would talk with my fellow comics fans and we would debate who would crush whom in some imaginary battle, we were the ones doing the fighting in our imaginations, the particular powers of our favorite characters having reflected part of our images of ourselves, the range of comics available granting us a space in which to explore our becoming as a group.

The individual monthly issues gave me moments of grounding in a world that we (myself, the writers/artists/publishers, and the other fans) were in the process of creating. And when the last page of an issue was turned, and the cover closed, the heroes would again enter my dreams and shape the inner reality of my child mind. I would put on my cape and wander down to the dock at dawn, and when the fog appeared, it didn't just roll in—it was summoned, and I was the magician with the mystical eye controlling the world.

For me, as a child, this relationship was not only with the characters but with the world they inhabited (called the Marvel Universe).† That world had clearly defined physical laws (including interdimensional spaces, multiple realities, divine beings, magical sciences, etc.) and, as important, a clearly defined ethical perspective (to my adult mind defined by Uncle Ben's ethic that "with great power there must also come great responsibility"‡) and deep understanding of outsiderhood, to which I related very fully. With every reading, that world opened again, and buying comics was a vital part of that experience. I always knew there would be a return to the Marvel Universe that I could look forward to, and all I had to do was take my two-dollar allowance to the soda shop (the issues cost 25 cents at that time, so I could always get eight).

So you see, the experience of the superhero in my case had a number of important elements: a price of admission, a place of purchase, a type of reader, a type of character, a set of friends to talk to about the experience and compare heroes with, and particular places for the reading (I remember a specific room in our summer camp especially). These combined to create a whole that was uniquely mine.

All of us who read comics and enjoy thinking about superheroes will have a set of elements like these, unique to his or her experience, that shades the meaning of the superhero and brings depth, breadth, and complexity to it. The superhero as a cultural phenomenon then bridges these isolated encounters and provides both a cultural context for them and a consistent element, the cultural artifact (the numbered issue

---

* Editors' note: "Stan's Soapbox" was the title of the editorial column written by Stan Lee that appeared in all of Marvel's comic books.
† All the superheroes published by a company, such as Marvel or DC, are considered to live in the same universe and can interact with each other.
‡ Uncle Ben is Peter Parker's (Spider-Man's) father fi gure.

or the film), that embeds the superhero, packaging the experience and allowing us access to it.

To further our phenomenological analysis, each of the elements from all our individual experiences could be further explored, allowing us to develop a much more refined sense of the overall meaning of the superhero for our culture (whatever that might be). In this way phenomenology helps us look at meanings across a variety of scales in time and place. For example, in the brief history I gave earlier, we have the experience of Captain Marvel and Dr. Strange at a summer camp in Lake Linden, Michigan, in the years 1970 to 1974, a relatively specific time and place that was extremely isolated from the mainstream, a seven-hour drive from any large town. The experience was characterized by a child's imagination, by a sense of mystery (the comics themselves being sort of underground, with few readers in my area, etc.), and by a social context as well (being a comics fan was an outsider activity).

When I went to the spinner rack to buy these comics, they were new, and the artists and writers were working for a smallish company with a very devoted readership that was reflected in the style of the letters to the editor and in Stan's Soapbox. There was a clear "we/they" opposition of Marvel against DC Comics. Further, the spinner rack was an add-on to the real purpose of the business of the soda shop where I bought my issues, which was selling food. Thus the rack was a kind of hidden gem, and this gave it an air of mystery, a kind of "how did this get there?" feeling that I relished as a 6- or 7-year-old buyer. Of course, my height was an issue; I didn't top the rack then, and the comic books would have seemed bigger because of this.

Phenomenology is built on descriptions like this that allow us to access the hidden points of the experience, the parts that don't register at first. For example, I'd forgotten the amazing sense of discovery: this was my first encounter with comics of any kind. They were pure magic, and they had a smell of newness when I picked them up from their slots on the rack. There were maybe 20 possibilities in that rack, and over the months of buying I had to winnow those down to find the heroes who meant something to me. So the process was of elimination and refining of taste. No Sgt. Rock for me!* I can even remember that sometimes when I was sick my dad would pick comics up for me to cheer me up, and he always came home with the wrong ones; World War II combat did nothing for me at the time. Those guys weren't superheroes, though I read their stories. They were too mundane for me.

In looking at the spinner rack this way, the importance of the purchase context to the experience of the superhero becomes, I hope, clear. It sets the stage and is the first step in the encounter both with the superheroes and with their corporate/consumer system. When I was a kid, the soda shop owner was Old Mr. Lindell, who clearly thought the comics were a little weird, though he was happy they brought in a little extra cash to the business. And I'm sure he thought all us comics customers were incipient hooligans. This made the superhero part of an underground and gave me a feeling of belonging, as did the manner of Marvel promotions at the time.

---

* Sgt. Rock was a DC character, a non-commissioned officer in World War II.

All the other elements of the experience of the superhero have similar value in creating the overall experience and bear both description and phenomenological analysis to help their part in the definition become clear. Further, once one has done the preliminary thinking, the history of the experience emerges as one compares the style of an element at different times in life.

For example, as an adult reader I no longer go to a soda shop for my comics fix; instead I use my local comics shop or eBay, and this is a totally different kind of superhero encounter. The comics shop has huge posters, life-sized cardboard cutouts of comics characters, and amazing toys that are sculpturally beautiful to see. This setting moves the experience from the fringe (a few issues in spinner rack in a town at the edge of nowhere) to the mainstream (a shop totally devoted to my kind of people). Not only do these additional features make the place differently enjoyable to visit, but they imply the transformations in the corporate context of superheroness: there's more money in the business, and that lets me know that the mainstream has opened and that comics have become cool. The salesperson is no longer a curmudgeonly old man; instead he's an ultimate comics geek, a virtual reference for all things superhero (and beyond). Thus the experience opens to conversation in a new way, and my understanding of the superhero and its definitions grows. Conversations like this, with people as knowledgeable and enthusiastic as oneself, change the experience: you don't sneak in as you did when the comics were underground; instead, you're invited. You get asked what you like, and then there's help finding the new that fits. In this way you could say I've moved from the cosmic consciousness of the early 1970s and the edgier, hipper X-mania of the 1980s and 1990s and have found myself invited into the world of the *Ultimates** we're in today.

I hope that you will take a moment and give yourself the treat of a phenomenological tour of your own experience of superheroness, isolating its elements and describing them as fully as possible. Overall, for myself, I find at the heart of my many years' experience a mix of nostalgia for my old way of reading and a deeper and more complex understanding of the medium itself that has been rewarding. I can no longer go out on the dock and semi-believe that if I raise my hands the clouds will roll in at my bidding. That's a big loss for me, and I still collect the old issues my mom threw away, hoping to bring it back. On the other hand, I have grown with the world I loved as a child, and I have come to understand the ins and outs of the art and the business in a way that has added depth to my enjoyment of comics and superheroes as a whole.

---

* Over the past few years, Marvel has been revisiting many of its old characters and stories but is placing them in modern time (versus decades ago when they were originally created); the collection of these revisited characters and stories is referred to as a character's *Ultimate* series: for example, *Ultimate Spider-Man*.

TEN

What Is a Superhero? No One Knows—That's What Makes 'em Great

Geoff Klock

Geoff Klock, an assistant professor at the Borough of Manhattan Community College, received his doctoral degree in English literature from Oxford University. Among the courses he teaches is literary criticism. He is the author of *How to Read Superhero Comics and Why*. Marvel Comics writer Matt Fraction named a villain after him: the killer Dokkktor Klockhammer.

I once got a drunken call from my brother-in-law, who was at a party, apparently hip-deep in some kind of semi-heated debate about whether or not Batman was a superhero. Some *idiot* had taken the position that Batman was not a superhero, because he had no powers, and some *reasonable* person was about to punch him. My brother-in-law had called me, his local superhero expert, to adjudicate. I think I said something about how being "rich" within the world of superhero comics means, for all intents and purposes, unlimited funding, and that it basically counts as a power. But I knew that was not very satisfying. The real reason I thought Batman was a superhero was because he just *was*.

If you took Philosophy 101 back in the day, and if your teacher was any good at all, you will remember a famous problem that comes up when studying Plato's Theory of Forms. Plato believed in two worlds: the "true" world, in which all objects and ideas exist in their actual, perfect forms, and the earthly world (i.e., our world), which is merely a poor reflection of that Higher, Heavenly World of Truth, Beauty, and Goodness. Physical love on earth is a poor excuse for Pure Heavenly Love, of which it is, for Plato, merely a lowly example, not the "real deal"—which is why a "Platonic relationship" is one in which no sex is involved. Crummy earthly justice is as close as we get to True Heavenly Justice down here. Earthly justice participates in this Eternal Form of Justice, but it does not work perfectly because it is too far away from the real thing. How do we know anything about this Eternal Form of Justice? By extrapolating from the earthly examples of justice in, say, courtrooms.

You see the problem? You need to know what Heavenly Justice is in the first place to know whether the verdict in the O. J. Simpson murder trial is an example of it. But you need the O. J. verdict, among others, to begin to guess what Heavenly Justice looks like, because earthly examples are the only way to apprehend Heavenly Forms. And round and round we go. The same problem applies to superhero comics. To get at a definition of "superhero," you need examples, but without a proper definition of "superhero," how do you know whether the characters you want to use as examples of superheroes are superheroes in the first place?

The thing is, I do not want to shortchange the emotional attachments I have built in a lifetime of reading comics. I don't want to have to say, "Batman is not a superhero," and I certainly don't want to have to say it in service of some merely academic argument that these guys over here are superheroes, while these other guys over there are not. At the heart of DC's superhero comics, you have to have Superman, Batman, and Wonder Woman. Period. The heart of Marvel's superhero comics has to embrace the Fantastic Four and Spider-Man, as well as the Avengers, whose ranks include Captain America, Thor, and Iron Man. These are, to my mind, Gospel Facts. I think any definition of "superhero" that leaves out any of these characters is going to be totally unacceptable. You can make the argument that some of these guys are not superheroes, and your argument might be totally solid, but it is going to have no pragmatic effect. It is not going to catch on, because anyone who cares enough to listen is already in too deep to exclude any of these characters from the definition of "superhero." It would be throwing the baby out with the rocket fuel that brought him to Kansas.

So let's try to start from this core group. Superman is an alien with alien powers, Batman is a regular guy with realistic but advanced technology and a big budget, and Wonder Woman is from a magic island and has a magic lasso. Captain America is a soldier whose body has been augmented through science, Thor is a god, and Iron Man is a guy with realistic but advanced technology and a big budget. The Fantastic Four and Spider-Man have been given powers by exposure to radiation and a radioactive spider bite, respectively. Aliens, regular dudes with advanced technology, magic and gods, humans mutated by radiation—this is pretty diverse. This is going to be hard to get a definition out of. With Batman and Iron Man, and arguably Captain America, having innate "superpowers" is not going to be a defining characteristic.

They all fight crime and save people. They have that in common. But lots of ordinary folks fight crime and save people. Police officers, firefighters, and Good Samaritans are not considered superheroes, even when using good technology or being well funded. Many touching 9/11 comics made the argument that these real folks *are* superheroes, but this kind of hagiography will water down our definition too much. We need a specific definition. As Syndrome, the bad guy in *The Incredibles*, put it, when everyone is special, no one will be.

Hiding one's identity while fighting crime and saving people is a tempting criterion. A lot of the individuals on our core list of superheroes do that, mostly. And our guys also take the law into their own hands, mostly. But a hidden identity cannot be the defining characteristic, nor can taking the law into one's own hands. The Ku Klux Klan did both, and we do not want to consider them superheroes. Marvel's Fantastic Four do neither, mostly.

"Mostly" keeps getting us into trouble. These characters have long histories and experience constant change at the hands of a dizzying host of writers and editors. And it was the constant change of the earthly world that made Plato so gung-ho about those Eternal Forms—the Essence that stayed the same underneath all that horrible, unpredictable change. But I do not think we are obligated to join Plato in his Church of Eternal Definitions. I don't think we have to join his battle against The Horrors of Change. I think we can say there is no Platonic Essence of the Superhero without falling into the despair of the religious who need something eternal to rely on. I think we can embrace the wild and unruly forces that Christianity, Plato, and the search for a good definition try to defend us against. Let's not make an argument that Superman, Batman, Wonder Woman, Thor, Captain America, Iron Man, Spider-Man, and the Fantastic Four are or are not superheroes. Kicking some key characters out of the heart of the genre to make a technical point about a definition might give us a kind of religious-style certainty, but it does not seem to be a good trade in my book. We lose more than we get. Police and legal procedurals are clearly defined, but their definitions do not make the stories they have to tell better, nor do they help in the critical evaluation of why those stories matter.

In fact, I think a good definition of "superhero" would actually *obscure* why superheroes matter. The consequences of the impossibility of defining "superhero" are too juicy to give up, and are at the very center of the greatness of the superhero. If you can't say what a superhero is, then you can't say what characteristics do not belong in any given story that features Batman, for example. Christopher Nolan may imagine him as a realistic vigilante who drives a tank through the streets, but in the hands of other writers, Batman employs shark repellant spray, visits other planets, and punches telepathic gorillas in the crotch.

Other genres do not work like this. A legal drama cannot take place in space without its being considered primarily a science fiction show and being judged as such. The comparison is between *Battlestar Galactica* and *Star Trek*; the trial of Gaius Baltar in *Battlestar Galactica* is never seriously compared to an episode of *Law and Order*, and a show like *Law and Order: Space Crimes* is never going to exist. Superheroes are not bounded by any such rules, and that is awesome. You can do whatever you want in a superhero story, and it still gets to be a superhero story.

You can even have a superhero story that explicitly tells you it is *not* a superhero story. At the start of his run on the *New X-Men* comic book, author Grant Morrison exploited the unclear boundaries of superhero comics as he very aggressively chucked the whole "superhero" label out the window. In his first issue, Morrison suddenly replaces the X-Men's usual colorful and diverse costumes with hardcore and hip matching black leather street gear. The Beast says, when the team is asked for their thoughts on the new school uniforms, "I was never sure why you had us dress up as superheroes anyway, Professor." Cyclops, ever the good student, answers, "The Professor thought people would trust us more if we looked like something they understood." So it is not just that Morrison's X-Men no longer see themselves as superheroes. Cyclops is asserting here that they never were superheroes. It is a shocking and disturbing and wonderful moment that *works* because Morrison knows what I am talking about here. With no definition of the superhero, on what basis are you going to disagree with Cyclops?

Superhero comics, even at their worst, have, because of their lack of boundaries, the ability to tell singularly bizarre stories—potential realized in a host of gorgeously contradictory tales that make up the fictional history of some of the genre's main characters. A post on the *Comics Alliance* blog[1] points out that audacious nonsense is at the heart of the most famous superhero characters. Here is author Chris Sims's technically accurate description of the X-Men's Wolverine:

> In the Core Marvel Universe, the most popular person is a 120 year-old [*sic*] Canadian berserker samurai who has who has [*sic*] been to the moon and was in love with a psychic who destroyed an alien planet and came back from the dead, married to both Japanese royalty and a green-haired terrorist, and had a child with a woman from a hidden region of Antarctica where dinosaurs and cavemen live. When he is not fighting his enemies—most of whom are versions of himself, some of whom have claws made of lasers—he reaffirms his status as a tough-as-nails loner as a member of at least three superhero teams.

Here is the equally unarguable summary of Spider-Man's most famous opponent, the Green Goblin:

> In the Core Marvel Universe, the flagship character's girlfriend was tragically killed when she was thrown off a bridge by an industrialist on a flying piece of sheet metal who later died, but came back and killed an alien queen in the head on television. This man . . . is now the defacto head of Homeland Security.

Here is Sims's account of Thor:

> In the Marvel Universe, Thor—the literal Norse god of Thunder—was turned into a frog for three issues, including one where his magic hammer turned him into a 6′6″ frog-man (er, frog-god), which had the side effect of chipping his hammer so that another frog (who had once been a man before he was cursed by a fortune-teller) could turn into a normal-sized frog-god, which came in handy when he had to team up with a teleporting dog and a saber-toothed tiger to get magic gems back from an alien from Jupiter's moon who was in love with the living embodiment of Death.

It is my claim that superhero comics do not have clear definitions, and it is my claim that we, as comic book academics, should keep it that way, so that we will continue to accept the kinds of stories, in all their strangeness, summarized by *Comics Alliance*. Lunacy is truly what makes superhero comics great. If you read comics, you know that *all* the big superheroes can be described with stories like the ones above. To say superheroes must have superpowers would push Batman out of the genre. If they must have a secret identity, then The Fantastic Four are gone. If magic makes a story part of the genre of fantasy, then there goes Wonder Woman and Thor. If aliens are for science fiction, Superman is out. Even a straightforward definition such as "all superheroes must fight supervillains" would force us to abandon Paul Chadwick's lovely *Concrete*, which tells the story of a man transformed by aliens into a creature of living stone; he does not face anything out of the ordinary after that, though he does try to help regular people with his new abilities. We could label the X-Men's Wolverine as a science fiction character, rather than a superhero, but it is the slamming together of superhero, science fiction, fantasy, samurai, and hard-boiled crime that makes that character what he is.

There is a larger argument here, outside the scope of this chapter, that no genre needs a strict definition—that genres are nothing more than convenient labels used to help businesses like Amazon.com sort things, labels readers know have severe limits, labels writers gleefully ignore and shred and recombine as they create such masterpieces as *Samurai Jack*, *Firefly*, *Dark City*, *Scott Pilgrim*, *From Dusk till Dawn*, *Brick*, and *Punch Drunk Love*. It has been said that if you accept the superhero worlds of Marvel and DC as huge continuous narratives, then they might be some of the largest single stories in human history. It also makes them the biggest genre mash-ups ever, and thus the most resistant to a clear definition.

If we are going to try to define the superhero, someone is going to have to show me that it is possible, and desirable; someone is going to have to show me the upshot, and that person is going to have to do better than the stories summarized above—or at least do them no damage, by, say, telling me some of them are not "really" superhero stories. No easy feat, though I am willing to listen.

NOTES

1. Chris Sims, "True Stories of the 'Core Marvel Universe.' " *Comics Alliance*. Laura Hudson, Editor. November 24, 2009. http://www.comicsalliance.com/2009/11/24/true-stories-of-the-core-marvel-universe

Superheroes Need Supervillains

Superheroes don't only battle everyday criminals or alien intruders; they also battle foes who challenge the superheroes' powers to the maximum and who force superheroes to make tough choices, choices that continually lead the costumed crusaders to be selfless, to sacrifice something in order to help other people. The foes who put superheroes in this position are more than villains—they are supervillains. As the essays in this section explore, supervillains play an integral part in defining the superhero and the genre.

ELEVEN

Why Supervillains?

Paul Levitz

Paul Levitz is in the unique position of looking at comics from a variety of vantage points: as an avid fan during his high school years (during which time he co-wrote and published a comics fan magazine), as a comic book writer, as an editor, as an executive (rising to President and Publisher of DC Comics), and as a scholar, expressed both in his more recent written work (such as *75 Years of DC Comics: The Art of Modern Mythmaking*) and through his teaching as an adjunct faculty member at Columbia University, Pace University, and at Manhattanville College.

Truly great superheroes are built to endure, and that means a constant stream of challenges must await them, more varied than the Labors of Hercules, more dangerous than the Perils of Pauline, and more emotionally moving than the unending cascade of cases on the gurneys of *E.R.*

It's possible for ordinary heroes to have long-lasting careers facing ordinary adversaries or ordinary problems or puzzles. In diverse media, the hero's triumph over a challenge or solution of a knotty dilemma is important enough if the reader or viewer can't solve it before the hero does. There are master villains for some heroes—for example, Moriarty for Holmes—but not true supervillains, because the ultimate humanity of the heroes can be stretched to its limit by very human villains. The master villain is more dangerous than a typical human, because his or her skills are passionately bent in a dangerous direction, but less dangerous than the supervillain, who is gifted with inhuman abilities and chooses a selfish path to exploit them. In the absence of a super-powered protagonist, there's no need for a super-powered villain—and certainly not for a parade of them.

For instance, the tamest superhero stories do not revolve around villains at all, but around dilemmas that have no obvious resolution available by use of the hero's powers. Superman was particularly susceptible to such situations in his original television incarnation after its first season: how would he convince the blind girl that he truly was a super being, or how could he recover his memory after saving Earth from a collision with a Kryptonite asteroid? Stories like these help establish the humanity of archetypal superheroes (and were producible on early television budgets with primitive special effects), but they tend to reduce the stature of the character. And the stories of lesser heroes, such as the Elongated Man (whose adventures were short stories in the back of the Flash's comic), were designed to allow the reader to be intrigued by the puzzles they faced without feeling like much of anything was at stake.

It was possible to make these stories more colorful without supervillains by introducing more complex fantasy elements and by making the environments in which the heroes worked more immersive. The Superman comics of the 1960s were immensely successful with very few supervillains, but with an endless stream of super-powered guest stars, animals, or transformations that made for distinctive visuals that might intrigue the reader (why *has* Superman's head been changed to that of a giant ant?). When American comics were intended for children, these stories leaped from the newsstands.

Escalating the scale of danger, many superhero adventures involved basically faceless or generic criminals committing small-scale crimes. Sometimes the environment of the crime served to make it feel more fantastic (Batman regularly featured battles on gigantic props, as in a chase across the keys of a typewriter the size of a small house). Diverting as they were for young readers, few of these tales were memorable.

Stepping fully into the fantastic, many superheroes seemed to work in structures driven by the monster (or alien) of the day. It's a time-honored formula, driving many comics of the 1950s and extending into other media, with examples such as the first season of *Smallville* on television in the 21st century, which was structured around a Kryptonite-transformed human episode after episode. The menace from these monsters was greater (surely these were opponents that mere mortals couldn't defeat), and sometimes there was an element of moral dilemma (e.g., "must I kill to save others?"), but the conflict was still more physical than emotional.

So how, then, to escalate the drama to make it worthy of true superheroes, particularly as the audience for their adventures became older (in the case of comic book readers, steadily from the 1960s to the end of the 20th century) or more sophisticated in their tastes? The answer was found in an increasing presence of supervillains.

First, the supervillain provided the potential for a layered problem: rather than a simple obstacle for the hero to overcome or a puzzle for him or her to solve, the supervillain could repetitively pose difficulties of increasing scale and drama. There was now an antagonist who existed for the creation of ever more complicated situations. Longer stories became possible, and moments when the superhero could fail prior to a later triumph increased the roller-coaster-like excitement.

Second, the supervillain provided a worthier opponent for the superhero; armed with powers equal (or even superior) to those of the superhero, the supervillain was able to engage in physical combat with the hero that was more visually interesting, as well as more dramatic. Superman spent the 1940s and 1950s without a villain who could take his punch and return it; consider if that had been true in the career of a boxer or an athlete. By the 1960s, the Fantastic Four had faced off against Galactus, who literally devoured worlds for nourishment. Contests are simply more exciting between more evenly matched contenders, or when you're rooting for an underdog against the odds.

Third, the introduction of personal malice increased the characters' motivations and even genuine evil in the stories, making the hero's journey more heroic as he or she triumphed over these forces. Simply a "mad scientist" in his first incarnation, Lex Luthor evolved into a genius who blamed Superman for the childhood loss of his hair and ensuing humiliations, and then into a brilliant billionaire industrialist, driven to prove that his human mind was Earth's ideal, rather than Superman's alien physicality. This trend toward personal malice perhaps culminated in "Born Again," Frank Miller and David Mazzucchelli's classic 1986 *Daredevil* arc, in which the Kingpin systematically devastates every aspect of the hero's life, from his career to his personal relationships.

The combined effect of all these elements was to make the hero greater and more interesting, and to provide readers with more tension as they read the stories. As supervillains moved the central conflicts of stories beyond whether the superhero could prevent the robbery of a bank or jewelry store (all probably insured, anyway) or halt a monster's rampage through a city (which seemingly employed the fastest and most effective rebuilding crews imaginable, as no damage would be visible an issue later), the risks increased and the emotional motivations rose. Instead of facing the mindless menaces of Scylla and Charybdis*, our latter-day Odysseus could face the wiles of Circe, as we wondered whether her seduction would bring about his downfall. It simply made for a better story.

As a fringe benefit, supervillains provide a visual shorthand for the excitement within comics, offering the opportunity for more varied covers, as a procession of gaudily clad, stunningly powerful malefactors attracts instant attention. Creating an intriguing question in the reader's mind ("how will the superhero deal with his latest strange transformation?") gave way to the simple directness of a fight card: tonight, Batman versus the Joker, in a rematch worthy of the Thrilla in Manila. When comics are translated to film, the cover becomes the key art of a poster, with dueling power figures poised to battle, or for television, the shorthand power shows up in the glorious simplicity of a logline.

Pull up your ringside seat, cheer for your hero, and jeer the villain. It's going to be a super match tonight—no merely human fighters welcome any more.

* Editors' note: Scylla and Charybdis refer to mindless twin dangers to ships passing the narrow Strait of Messina: a towering huge rock (Scylla) and a whirlpool (Charybdis). The strait was narrow enough that sailors often were unable to steer their ships safely between them.

TWELVE

Superheroes Need Supervillains

Frank Verano

Frank Verano is a doctoral researcher in film studies at the University of Sussex. His research locates spaces of utopia and aspirational politics in the American direct cinema film cycle through an analysis of works by D.A. Pennebaker, David and Albert Maysles, Robert Frank, and Bob Dylan. His work in comics studies, on comics and consumption and Grant Morrison and Situationist Theory, has been presented at conferences and published in the *International Journal of Comic Art*.

You either die a hero, or live long enough to see yourself become the villain.

When district attorney Harvey Dent uttered this line in *The Dark Knight* (2008), he had no idea what fate had in store for him. First a heroic public servant, then a ruthless supervillain, Dent—later, Two-Face—is a living embodiment of the film's exploration of the line that separates a hero from a villain. And, as we will see, sometimes that line is a thin one. Superheroes and supervillains sometimes coexist in a somewhat symbiotic relationship, in an almost brutal choreography around this "line." The social identity of both heroes and villains is very much informed by and defined by their opposition to each other, which justifies their very existence within the social fabric of the superhero story.

GAZING INTO THE BLACK MIRROR

Why do superheroes need supervillains, anyway?

Most obviously, the supervillain is there to make the hero look good. It is often said that a hero is defined by his villains, and it is abundantly clear that a strong villain makes for an even stronger superhero. Supervillains that represent broad, base evils are a standard conceit of the superhero genre; when a figure that represents absolute evil is defeated, the absolute good of the superhero is glorified and his or her role in society is justified. Many superhero comics feature an archenemy, that villain who acts as the hero's doppelganger—his or her mirror opposite. Where would Batman be without the Joker, or Professor X without Magneto?

The archenemy represents an inversion of the hero's values and is a figure with whom the hero is constantly at odds—physically, mentally, and ideologically—providing another opportunity for the superhero to look good. The Green Goblin, for example, is a supervillain born out of old, paranoid, "bad" science that perverts the optimistic, youthful, "good" science that Spider-Man embodies. Many times, this conflict even plays out in a character's visuals—the acid-drenched, devil's-jester look of the Joker drowns out the drab, gothic Batman, and the rigid, industrialized

Dr. Doom is constantly at odds with the pliable Mr. Fantastic. Nothing demonstrates the exemplary values of the superhero quite as effectively as the never-ending battle of comic book good versus evil, in which those values are constantly challenged but reaffirmed upon the villain's defeat. The villain's negative qualities highlight the hero's positive ones.

The relationship between Superman and his famous archenemy Lex Luthor is perpetually fascinating to fans because the characters represent, respectively, the very best and very worst in humanity. As *All-Star Superman* author Grant Morrison comments, "Superman is us at our best, Luthor is us when we're being mean, vindictive, petty, deluded and angry . . . . It's like a bipolar/manic-depressive personality*—with optimistic, loving Superman smiling at one end of the scale and paranoid, petty Luthor cringing on the other."[1] Both figures represent male power fantasies, but Luthor is the fantasy ideal turned sickly and diseased. "We have to recognize them both as potentials within ourselves," claims Morrison. "It's essential to find yourself rooting for Lex, at least a little bit, when he goes up against a man-god armed only with his bloody-minded [sic] arrogance and cleverness."[2] To Luthor, Superman's mere existence denigrates human accomplishment. He never had to work for his superstrength or other abilities. Still, for all his ingenuity, resourcefulness, and championing of the human spirit, Luthor's petty obsession and narcissism never allow him to use his abilities to better the humanity he claims to be defending. While selfish and angry feelings are perfectly natural aspects of being human, Luthor demonstrates that, taken to an extreme, they can be antisocial, self-defeating, and flat-out mean. Instead, the reader is encouraged to aspire to the compassionate and humanist Superman, whose exemplary moral code is the very opposite of Luthor's. Superman can be portrayed as the ultimate potential of humanity only if he's constantly being challenged by elements that represent it at its worst.

If superheroes and their archenemies are represented as two sides of the same coin, what, then, separates them? Fate? Circumstance? The archenemy offers the hero a sobering reminder of "what might have been." Superheroes are often the product of socially advantageous situations—a loving family, strong role models, economic stability—that heavily inform the hero's ability to find positive motivation to use his or her abilities for good after a set of tragic circumstances instead of falling into despondency, despair, and evil. In a way, the supervillain, who lacks these circumstantial advantages, continually reminds the hero of the good fortune that put him or her on a socially positive path. Had fate been less kind, perhaps the superhero would actually be a supervillain.

---

* Editors' note: Morrison's metaphoric use of "bipolar/manic-depressive personality" is not an accurate representation of the underlying phenomenon he seems to be describing. Bipolar disorder involves an alternation of significantly different mood states, rather than, as Morrison describes it, a continuum of personality traits.

In *Batman: The Killing Joke* (1988), writer Alan Moore and artist Brian Bolland recount the Joker's possible origin, in which a failed career as a comedian, petty crime, a freak accident that kills his wife and unborn child, and a fall into a batch of toxic chemicals swirl into a nightmarish stew that births the Clown Prince of Crime. As Batman hunts the Joker through a dilapidated circus that resembles the accumulation of a lifetime of bad trips, the Joker realizes the two foes have a common starting point. He asks Batman, "You had a bad day once, am I right? I know I am. I can tell. You had a bad day and everything changed. Why else would you dress up like a flying rat?"[3] The difference, of course, is the path that each man chose in coming to terms with his "one bad day." The more privileged Batman adopted the mantle of the bat to channel his war on crime through a symbol precisely to prevent himself from going insane after witnessing the murder of his parents as a child, as the Joker asserts he should have done. Batman's greatest social advantage over the Joker is likely Alfred Pennyworth, the Wayne family butler, whose morality, compassion, and presence as a strong role model in those highly formative years following his childhood trauma gave young Bruce a strong foundation through which to channel his reaction to his parents' death. In contrast, the Joker—who had no such social supports—"snapped" after his series of traumatic events and was reborn as an agent of chaos, terror, and fear who sought to inflict his skewed vision of the world as an irrational, absurd joke upon Gotham City.

ESCALATION

The supervillain gives legitimacy to the superhero's mission. In Christopher Nolan's *Batman Begins* (2005), Batman operates outside the law as a wanted vigilante to take on the mob, a supervillainous psychiatrist (the Scarecrow), and an eco-terrorist (Ra's al Ghul). By the film's conclusion, he has forged a level of trust with Lieutenant Jim Gordon, who calls upon him when a case goes beyond what typical police are equipped to handle—the next supervillain attack in Gotham by the Joker. As criminal activity escalates into more dangerous and terrifying super-crime, so, too, must the forces of justice ramp up their efforts if they are to combat it. In the sequel film *The Dark Knight*, Batman is still regarded as an illegal vigilante to be arrested on sight, but off the record his nighttime activities are tolerated, encouraged, and often conducted with the cooperation of Gordon and the district attorney. Had Gotham not been plagued with supercriminals, or "freaks," as they are referred to in the films, would there have been a place for Batman in a world of cops and mobsters?

In a way, supervillains give superheroes a reason to exist and function in a given society. When supervillains disrupt order, superheroes restore it. By their very nature, superheroes are reactive. They preserve the status quo and rid the system of radical supercriminal elements. However, what would happen if there were no supervillains? What if a superhero lived in a world where supervillains either did not exist or were completely vanquished? What happens when a superhero gets proactive?

THE "POST-SUPERVILLAIN" SUPERHERO—HIS OR HER
OWN WORST ENEMY?

The "proactive superhero" was a popular theme in comics at the turn of the 21st century, but variations on this theme abound throughout comics history. Interestingly, these stories usually operate under the same principles and work toward the same conclusion, time and again. It has been said that supervillains justify the superhero's mission and give him or her a socially approved space within which to act. Without supervillains, it is difficult to justify the hero's reason for being. In *Miracleman*, one of Alan Moore's earliest "big statements" on superheroes, we are witnesses to "what comes next" after the arch-villain's final defeat. Miracleman assembles his superhuman allies, and together they swiftly depose all world governments and impose totalitarian rule over the entire planet. From their god-like perspective, they have created a utopia, but the view from below is not quite as rosy. In *Superman: Red Son* (2003), writer Mark Millar and artist Dave Johnson craft a story in which Superman is raised in the Soviet Union at the height of the Cold War. As Premier of the Soviet Union, Superman uses his super-abilities to create a utopia under his totalitarian rule, but he suffers a breakdown when he realizes that, in imposing his will where he has no right, he is no better than the supervillains he used to fight. In both of these stories, superheroes, though they have the best intentions, become their own worst enemies. The void left by the absence of supervillains frees up the superhero to pursue a new role; suddenly, the hero is not spending all of his time responding to supercrimes. He has agency and can examine the structures in society that create crime, and he can put a stop to crime before it happens. Still, as Superman wonders in *Red Son*, what gives him the right to decide for all of society?

In this regard, it might be argued that supervillains keep superheroes within their boundaries, as well. In the 2004 *Marvel Knights: Spider-Man* series, Millar cleverly introduces the idea that supervillains are the product of a military-industrial complex that wants to keep superheroes occupied with day-to-day conflicts to prevent them from enacting real social change. Looking at it this way, the superhero–supervillain relationship can be seen as a system of checks and balances. By continually clashing, keeping each other busy, and, effectively, cancelling each other out, a bizarre status quo is maintained that allows humanity to decide its own destiny.

In effect, the supervillain makes the superhero a superhero. The presence of supervillains creates the primary directive of the superhero narrative—the preservation of the status quo. Without the supervillain, the superhero morphs into a cause of social disruption that, taken to its natural progression, leads to the superhero becoming a supervillain. The proactive, progressive superhero is inevitably a problematic figure; good intentions aside, when a powerful figure forces societal change without the right to do so, he or she has entered supervillain territory.

NOTES

1. Quoted in Zack Smith, "All Star Memories: Grant Morrison on *All Star Superman*," *Newsarama*, October 7, 2008, http://www.newsarama.com/comics/100827-Morrison-Superman-05.html (October 1, 2011).
2. Smith, "All Star Memories," http://www.newsarama.com/comics/100827-Morrison-Superman-05.html.
3. Alan Moore. (1988). *Batman: The Killing Joke*. New York: DC Comics, p. 38.

THIRTEEN

Superheroes Need Superior Villains

Stanford W. Carpenter

Stanford W. Carpenter is a Culural Anthropologist, Chairman of the Board of Directors for the Institute for Comics Studies, and Assistant Professor in the Department of Visual and Critical Studies at the School of the Art Institute of Chicago. His ethnographic research focuses on the construction of community and identity from the perspective of creators and related professionals in various media organizations. His dissertation was an ethnography of comic book creators and companies. His work on comics includes "Truth Be Told: Authorship and the Creation of the Black Captain America" in *Comics as Philosophy*, "Black Lightning's Story" in *Third Person* and his upcoming book *The Work of Imagining Identity in Comic Books*. He looks at issues of identity and superheroes from the perspective of comic book creators and companies.

Superheroes need *superior* villains to raise the stakes of the heroic struggle by putting culturally defined value systems in high relief. A culturally defined value system is a mix of positive and negative values that correspond to responsibility and irresponsibility. Superheroes represent positive values by being responsible. While this may seem simple enough, responsibility is an ongoing internal struggle for superheroes. Simply put, power corrupts. Responsibility is the essential quality that distinguishes superheroes from regular villains. Being responsible, no matter the personal cost, is the superhero's only defense against being corrupted by power. Superheroes are thus defined, limited, and restrained by their struggle to be responsible, to exercise their abilities and power with restraint. Supervillains' lack of restraint and utter irresponsibility are a threat to the superhero, and to the people the superhero protects. But the superior villain is a much greater, more imminent threat. Whereas regular villains prey on, and therefore need, the structure and institutions of their society, superior villains both critique and threaten the positive values of the culture and society that the superhero represents. Superior villains are irresponsible actors who exercise their abilities and powers without restraint or concern for collateral damage. Superior villains challenge superheroes by externalizing their internal struggle to be responsible. It's never a fair fight.

WITH GREAT POWER COMES GREAT RESPONSIBILITY

Culturally defined value systems and notions of responsibility take on different dimensions when applied to different superheroes. Two superhero–superior villain pairs provide useful contrast: Professor X and Magneto, and Batman and the Joker.

Professor X is a mutant who struggles with the responsible use of his telepathic powers, which inherently circumvent free will, privacy, and various fundamental human rights, as well as definitions of what it is to be human. At the same time, Professor X tries to win the hearts and minds of humans and mutants in order to create a more tolerant and inclusive society within a human populace that hates and fears mutants. He has a superior villain counterpart—Magneto—who uses his own mutant power to further the cause of mutant rights at the expense of human lives.

Batman has nearly unlimited resources in his quest to bring law and order to Gotham City, but his personal rules of engagement—specifically, his code against killing and zero tolerance for collateral damage—limit his ability to address a superior villain, the Joker, committed to creating chaos and maximizing collateral damage.

SUPERIOR VILLAINS CHOOSE VIOLENCE OVER WINNING HEARTS AND MINDS: MAGNETO AS SUPERIOR VILLAIN TO PROFESSOR X

Professor X stands as a symbol of tolerance to be challenged by Magneto's intolerance in a world where mutants are discriminated against, hunted, persecuted, and killed by humans who hate and fear them. Professor X and Magneto are both mutants. In narratives that parallel various civil and human rights movements, both are advocates for mutant people. Professor X and Magneto are former friends whose split over ideological differences has made them mortal enemies. Professor X is commonly referred to as a dreamer, an optimist who believes in equality, diversity, and peaceful coexistence between humans and mutants. Professor X's superior villain is Magneto, a cynic and a terrorist who believes that the only way for mutants to be safe is through the violent takeover of mutantkind.

Professor X is the world's most powerful telepath. His powers include clairvoyance, mind control, mind reading, mental communication, and the ability to alter or erase memories and perceptions. The young people he trains, the X-Men, are mutants and outcasts who fight "to protect a world that hates and fears them."[1] But the fight is not just about saving the world; it is about showing the world that it does not have to fear mutants. Professor X's dream echoes Dr. Martin Luther King's dream of a world where people "will not be judged by the color of their skin but by the content of their character,"[2] or, in the case of mutants, the construction of their genome.

Professor X struggles with the responsible use of his telepathic powers in light of the positive values he represents: equality, free will, optimism, and tolerance. Yet his telepathic powers allow him literally to impose his will on others, know people's intentions, read their darkest thoughts, and violate their privacy. In matters where knowledge is power, where privacy matters, his telepathic abilities create situations of total inequality. If he were to use his telepathic powers to their full potential, he would become the very thing that he fights against.

Magneto has the ability to manipulate and control magnetic fields and possesses a helmet that renders him immune to all forms of telepathy. He is a Holocaust survivor who has seen the horrors of genocide firsthand; he draws a direct connection between the plight of Jews during World War II and the probable fate of mutants in a world of bigotry and hatred. He does not believe in peaceful coexistence; rather, he believes in the survival of *his people*—mutants (i.e., *Homo superior*). He is the ideological intersection of the phrases "never again"[3] and "by any means necessary,"[4] backed by sheer elemental power. He believes that the only way to prevent the genocide of mutants at the hands of humanity is to take the reins of power, no matter the cost in human lives.

Magneto externalizes Professor X's internal struggles as they relate both to his positive values and to the responsible use of his telepathic powers. Professor X is ideologically driven to make real an imagined future of peaceful coexistence and tolerance. Magneto's ideology is rooted in experiences and history that run counter to the future to that Professor X strives to realize. To the extent that Professor X represents a dream of the future, Magneto represents a view of reality, both past and present. As Professor X espouses the attainment of an idealized future, Magneto needs only to recall his past as a holocaust survivor, and the present-day persecution of mutants. The fact that Professor X can control minds creates suspicion as to whether his followers are acting of their own free will. Magneto is immune to mind control and has no mental powers, which allows him to state legitimately that he and his followers are acting of their own free will. And then there is Professor X's role as headmaster of a school of young mutants. Headmasters and teachers have a duty to educate and protect their students, yet Professor X trains students for combat and sends them into harm's way.

Unlike regular villains, but like superior villains, Magneto operates in the absence of internal conflict and restraint. He has declared total war on humanity and any mutants who protect humanity and therefore stand against their own kind. He does not teach students. Rather, he trains soldiers to subjugate, kill, and sacrifice in his name and for the cause of mutantkind, as he sees it.

SUPERIOR VILLAINS CHALLENGE ORDER WITH CHAOS: THE JOKER AS SUPERIOR VILLAIN TO BATMAN

Batman stands as a symbol of order that is challenged by the Joker's chaos. Batman is commonly referred to as "the Dark Knight," the crusading protector of Gotham City. Batman's superior villain is the Joker, a sociopathic criminal with access to countless disposable followers and weapons of mass destruction.

Batman's story begins when, as a child, he witnesses the senseless murder of his parents at the hands of a mugger. This child uses his inherited wealth to become Batman, a one-man police force with an unlimited budget to root out corruption while inspiring fear in the hearts of evildoers. Although Batman operates outside of the law, he has a rigid code against using guns and killing.

The Joker's true origins are shrouded in mystery. Often referred to as the Clown Prince of Crime, the Joker personifies a superior villain through his wanton destruction, utter lack of regard for human life, and pleasure in acts of killing and mass destruction. In short, the Joker is chaos to Batman's order. There is little logic behind the Joker's crimes outside of the satisfaction of destructive base desires and fatal whims. His weapon of choice is a toxin that literally makes people laugh until they die. He frequently uses bystanders and his own followers as human shields. The Joker's chaotic nature is in direct opposition to Batman's linear approach to establishing order.

The Joker draws Batman into a cycle that challenges the Caped Crusader's core values as they relate to justice and killing. The battle between Batman and the Joker ultimately boils down to a chase: Whenever Batman gets close to capturing the Joker, the Joker puts lives in jeopardy, which forces Batman to abandon his pursuit in order to save as many lives as he can while the Joker escapes. When Batman eventually captures the Joker, the Joker is inevitably judged to be criminally insane, put in an institution, and soon thereafter escapes to start the cycle of wanton death and destruction anew. Being criminally insane renders the Joker not responsible for his actions. Batman is often faced with a moment in this cycle when he could kill the Joker or, more commonly, let him die by failing to save him—as in the Joker's 1940 debut in *Batman* #1[5] or in the 2008 film *The Dark Knight*[6] —but he does not, thus creating the cycle. Within this dynamic, the cycle of putting the Joker in an institution only to have him escape and kill again calls Batman's code against killing into question as matter of practicality. Given Batman's history with the Joker, it also leads to the question of whether the blood of the Joker's victims is more appropriately put on the Batman's hands.

CONCLUSION

Superior villains are more powerful than superheroes because they play on the superheroes' inner conflicts, self-imposed limits, and fear that they might become what they oppose. Magneto uses his control of a fundamental force of nature to subjugate all who stand in his way. Professor X could do the same with a stray thought, but he doesn't because of his dedication to positive values. Magneto is a physical and psychological threat to Professor X. Magneto represents the temptations of power and moral shortcuts. Magneto uses his powers to chart the most direct (and often brutal) course toward his goals. Magneto forces Professor X to resist the temptation to use his telepathic abilities to chart an equally direct course. And therein lies the rub. Magneto has the benefit of ambiguity, of being seen by some as a terrorist and others as a freedom fighter. Magneto is redeemable. Professor X has to be unambiguously responsible in the use of his telepathic abilities precisely because his telepathic abilities have the potential to violate the fundamental human rights that he is fighting to achieve for mutants and undermine some of the basic definitions of what it is to be human, which mutancy itself puts into question. Professor X's internal struggle is more brutal than anything that Magneto could do in the physical world. Temptation—if he gives into it, he proves the case against mutantkind. Simply put, one mistake, one stray thought, a moment of irresponsibility, and Professor X is evil, beyond redemption.

Similarly, the Joker's penchant for wanton collateral damage forces Batman to relive perpetually the helplessness he felt as a child when he watched his parents' murders. But the only way Batman could truly end the cycle would be to become a killer, which would violate his dedication to positive values. The Joker's actions lead Batman to struggle with his dedication to positive values, to responsibility, in very real terms. Batman's crusade against evil necessitates that he work outside the law to establish order. His actions are brutal and violent. The only thing that distinguishes Batman as a superhero is his steadfast dedication to positive values, to justice, to responsibility.

The superior villain is not subject to the limits that responsibility imposes on the use of force. Magneto and the Joker have no qualms about killing, collateral damage, or sacrificing their followers. The combination of this lack of a broad sense of responsibility and their abilities makes the villains superior and their threat to the heroes more credible. At the same time, superior villains offer mystery, freedom, and alternative values that compete against the superhero's predictable, responsible, and normative values. It is not just a battle between good and evil; it's about responsibility (restraint) and freedom, winning the hearts and minds of the readers. Although Magneto might fight for mutants, he does so at the expense of humans, putting him in direct opposition to Professor X's dream. The Joker's penchant for chaos, mass destruction, and mass murder calls Batman's code against killing and zero tolerance for collateral damage into question.

The superior villain ups the stakes of the superhero's journey, often forcing the superhero to make personal sacrifices in order to maintain the values he or she represents, or else cease being a superhero. Professor X asks the people for whom he is responsible to sacrifice life and limb for his dream. At the same time, ethical concerns prevent him from fully exploiting his telepathic abilities in the service of his cause. Batman sacrifices his sense of self. Although he has access to incredible wealth and all of the benefits that come with it, his mission to bring order to Gotham City has so consumed his life that there is no room for a fully developed person when he takes off his mask.

The superior villain is superior to the superhero by virtue of not being constrained by the shackles of social responsibility and positive values. That's what makes the villain "free" and "cool"—the villain represents a certain vision of self-fulfillment and freedom from cultural norms. The victory of the superhero over the superior villain establishes and validates the cultural notions of responsibility embedded in the superhero's journey.

NOTES

1. Scott Lobell and Henry Clayton, "You Gotta Be Kidding." *Alpha Flight* 3.1, November 2004. New York: Marvel, p. 3.
2. Martin Luther King, Jr. (1992). "I Have a Dream." *I Have a Dream: Writings and Speeches*. San Francisco: Harper, p. 104.
3. Meir Kahan. (1972). *Never Again: A Program for Survival.* New York: Pyramid Books.
4. Malcolm X. (1992). *By Any Means Necessary.* New York: Pathfinder, p. vii.
5. Bob Kane and Bill Finger. *Batman #1*, Spring 1940. National Periodicals. New York, New York.
6. Christopher Nolan (Director). (2008). *The Dark Knight.* Warner Bros. Pictures. Burbank, California.

FOURTEEN

The Subjective Politics of the Supervillain

Chris Deis

Chris Deis is a doctoral student in political science at the University of Chicago and a lecturer at DePaul University who focuses on race and the politics of popular culture. He has published work on issues of race and representation in genre entertainment such as *Battlestar Galatica*, *Star Wars*, and *The Night of the Living Dead*.

In the popular imagination, the figure of the superhero evokes images of men and women with amazing powers wearing colorful costumes and having unbelievable adventures. These characters are also spectacular and utterly ridiculous: they can fly, shoot heat rays out of their eyes, have fantastic strength, are impervious to injury, or come from other planets. Ironically, it is these very traits that make them resonate with audiences. Because their abilities are so out of the ordinary, they are able to represent and embody deep truths about the human condition, truths that cut across culture, nation, and time. By implication, the superhero genre is about a great deal more than just guys and gals who wear tights and capes: these characters tell readers something about a given society's values, struggles, and beliefs.

Politics and popular culture are intertwined; they are not easily divided into neat, easily separable categories. Censorship, popular music, "Hollywood" and documentary films, style and fashion, and the ways that politicians are now also celebrities in the 24/7 news environment are all examples of "the popular" and "the political" overlapping. In all, popular culture is a barometer for the public mood and an informal type of public opinion. Superheroes and supervillains fit perfectly within this framework.

Definitions are central to the claims I advance in this chapter. For my purposes, the supervillain is "super" in a number of ways. Supervillains' powers are often rooted outside of their physical bodies—for example, as when character such as Kingpin leverages a criminal organization and minions to do his bidding.

Alternatively, supervillains might have the backing of governments, extensive financial resources, or a terrorist organization to support their machinations (Red Skull, The Mandarin, or Cobra Commander).[*] There are also supervillains who have

---

[*] All of these characters combine personal ambition with larger institutional and bureaucratic support in order to further their plans of world domination. Cobra Commander is the leader of a global terrorist network in the *G.I. Joe* comic book series. Red Skull, one of the recurring rivals of the iconic character Captain America, has either commanded or worked with the international terrorist organizations A.I.M. and Hydra in the long-running *Captain America* comic book series. The Mandarin is a key supervillain in the *Iron Man* comic book series (he has also appeared in other Marvel comics as well). He commands an international terrorist organization and "shadow government" with authority and resources that span the globe.

amazing abilities and powers, such as Darkseid or Apocalypse, while other supervillains such as Dr. Doom, Lex Luthor, or the Joker have genius-level intelligence and/or mastery of highly advanced science and technology.

The values of the supervillain are villainous in that they are antisocial and stand outside of the norms of "normal" society. Supervillains are also egomaniacal and selfish—personal enrichment, personal power, and control over others are their *raisons d'etre*. Supervillains are also committed to their goals, convinced of the justness of their cause, and unflappable in their beliefs. Consequently, their transgressions against the social order are never modest—rather, they are gross and spectacular.

These categories are all critical in our effort to understand superhero stories as a type of social commentary. The supervillain is not just a foil for the superhero. He or she is more than a character who happens to be a rival for the protagonist and who possesses equal or superior powers. While this definition is tempting, it is also quite incomplete.

In exploring how the characters in superhero stories can be viewed as political, I emphasize the following: supervillains are often also "super" in terms of their ambition, vision for the world, sense of grievance with the established authority, and understanding of the means and ends of "justice." In comparison to the superhero, the ways that supervillains embody these characteristics are both highly amplified and radically different.[*][1]

The various versions of the X-Men—whether in comics, film, or animated cartoons—are especially instructive in this regard, as they explicitly deal with questions of politics and identity. Born of the tumultuous 1960s, the X-Men stories have used "mutant" identity as a means to interrogate questions of personhood and citizenship critically as they relate to race, sexuality, class, gender, and physical disability. The X-Men (in their many varied iterations) are ultimately an extended meditation on difference and the challenges of living in a multicultural society in which discrimination and prejudice are not uncommon.

The leader of the X-Men is Professor X, a superpowered hero and an "integrationist." He believes humans and mutants can live together with mutual respect. The archvillain of the X-Men is Professor X's best friend turned rival, the supervillain Magneto, a mutant supremacist and separatist. While his powers are at least as great as those of Professor X, Magneto's ambition and vision are far greater, as is his sense of grievance with the wider world. Their relationship is one of the central tensions in the X-Men stories.

A survivor of the death camps and the Holocaust, Magneto has learned about humanity's capacity for barbarism and evil through painful and direct personal experience. Marked as the "Other" in Nazi-era Germany because he is Jewish, Magneto is also "racialized" by virtue of his mutancy. In contrast to Professor X, who grew up in a life of luxury and comfort, Magneto has come to understand that intolerance and hate are more the norms of human civilization than generosity and acceptance. Magneto's ambitions stand in direct proportion to his suffering.

Whereas the superhero Professor X seeks accommodation with "normal" humans, Magneto wants separation. Whereas Professor X sees a possibility for peaceful cohabitation,

---

[*] The idea of politics can be understood in a number of ways. For my purposes, politics is how a given society decides to allocate resources, the institutions put in place to do so, and how political elites and citizens negotiate these matters.

Magneto sees human exploitation of mutants. Professor X believes that a solution to the discrimination and hostility experienced by mutants can eventually be found. Magneto's vision demands that humans be obliterated; justice for mutants can demand nothing less in Magneto's experience. His "superior" set of grievances is mated with superpowers that mirror and rival those of the protagonists in the X-Men. In sum, Magneto possesses a grander social vision than Professor X, based on the political viewpoint that justice cannot be achieved through negotiation or accommodation.

My claim is not that all supervillains necessarily have a political ideology in the way that philosophers or political theorists would strictly define the concept. Magneto and other supervillains do not offer a coherent theory of politics that includes (1) an idea of how humankind behaves without and before government ("the state of nature") and (2) a clearly articulated vision of what the good society entails. The politics of supervillains are more likely to comprise a loose set of values and ideas that they embody as characters and want to see reflected in the world at large.

The ideology of the supervillain is base—it is a crude understanding of power and how best to attain it, a plan that is enabled and legitimated by a political narrative. Because the superhero and supervillain exist as mirrors of one another, the politics of the latter is further highlighted through comparison to the former. Superhero stories provide many examples. The Joker is a radical anarchist, whereas Batman stands for order and strong government. As offered above, Professor X is an integrationist liberal humanitarian, whereas Magneto is a mutant separatist and supremacist. In *Watchmen*, Ozymandias is a utopian megalomaniac and authoritarian, whereas the everyman "hero" Nite Owl believes in a democratic society. Inspired by the events of World War II, the superhero Captain America represents the virtues of an inclusive and democratic United States, whereas his rival the Red Skull is a Nazi fascist.

Up to this point I have suggested that superhero genre stories are political commentary, and the relationships of the characters—the superhero and the supervillain in this case—are examples of how popular culture can inform readers and audiences about deeper questions regarding identity, values, and politics in a society.[2] However, these claims have been based on an unstated assumption: the idea that superhero and supervillain are fixed and "real" categories. In discussions about the superhero genre, this language is used so casually that it is often not evaluated from a critical perspective. But upon review, these labels are wholly dependent on social context and one's own point of view.[3] For example, "terrorists" might be considered "freedom fighters" by their own people.* Historical "villains" such as Pol Pot, Osama Bin Laden, and Adolf Hitler might

---

* Historically there have been many "People's" or "liberation" struggles in which the legitimacy of the actors involved was framed by one's position relative to Power. In Algeria during the second half of the 20th century, for example, the indigenous guerrilla movement against the French was seen by many people around the world as an anti-colonial struggle against an unjust and imperial power. Conservatives in France considered the Algerian resistance fighters to be "criminals" and "terrorists" who dared to resist French authority. A second example can be drawn from the American Revolution, in which the colonials were viewed by the British as "traitors" in "revolt" against the legitimate authority of the Crown. By comparison, the colonials saw themselves as resisting "tyrannical" British rule.

be looked at as "evil" by their victims and bystanders, but their supporters might consider them icons of greatness. In the American context, figures such as Nat Turner, leader of a failed slave rebellion, and John Brown, a radical abolitionist, are viewed as heroic figures by black Americans, but they were reviled during their lifetimes by defenders of the Southern slaveocracy (and to this day remain unpopular among many white Americans).

Superhero narratives are relayed from a specific reference point. In the superhero genre, this reference point is not neutral; the narrative is usually framed to depict the hero in a sympathetic fashion, while the villain is shown less generously. The storytelling frame is also not omniscient: events are often alluded to in a story and are not directly depicted. The terms *superhero* and *supervillain* are particularly useful in this regard because they help the reader to make intuitive judgments and fill in the blanks about a story's direction, as well as the motivations driving the characters' behavior.

Here, context is integral to how readers follow the events in a story. When the context is changed and the reference point adjusted, the meaning taken away by the audience is altered. This is especially true with superheroes and supervillains. If the story is presented from the reference point of the supervillain, the story events take on another meaning. In essence, the categories of "superhero" and "supervillain" become inverted.

For example, in the 2006 graphic novel *Lex Luthor: Man of Steel*, the supervillain sees the superhero as a threat to society, possessing an exaggerated ego and in need of being restrained or roped in for the greater good.* In this story, Lex Luthor, archvillain and nemesis of Superman, is the protagonist. As such, the narrative is presented from the former's point of view. Superman is presented as an alien from another planet with powers that are greater than those of any "normal" human being. Ultimately, Superman is depicted as a looming threat to humankind because he is restrained only by his own impulses, whims, and desires. Lex Luthor imagines himself as the only person with the intelligence and courage to protect Earth and its people from the imminent threat posed by Superman's power.

As depicted in *Lex Luthor: Man of Steel*, what were initially noble and virtuous traits when presented from the point of view of the superhero become arrogant, judgmental, and often megalomaniac-like behaviors that are evidence of a "messiah complex" when seen from the supervillain's perspective. Likewise, the behaviors of the supervillain are now revealed to be reasonable and right, and the character comes to be presented in a sympathetic light as a "victim" of the "superhero's" harassment and violence.

This adjustment in how we use the language related to superheroes and supervillains is not a claim to a banal and empty type of moral relativism. Rather, it is a signal of how basic ideas about politics and justice are rooted in particular understandings that are neither universal nor absolute for all times and all people(s).[4] Because the superhero genre reflects a given society's values, it is subject to these questions of context. In all, the superhero is a rich site for exploring the politics of popular culture.

---

* *Lex Luthor: Man of Steel* (later collected as *Luthor*) was a five-issue limited series written by Brian Azzarello for DC comics in 2005.

Ironically, as we ask challenging questions about how the figures of the superhero and supervillain work as political commentary, it might in fact be the supervillain, and not the superhero, who reveals the most about foundational questions of power, politics, and identity.

NOTES

1. See Harold Lasswell. (1990). *Who Gets What, When, How.* New York: Peter Smith Publications.
2. There are several texts that are very helpful in detailing the relationships between popular culture and politics. For example, see John Street. (1997). *Politics and Popular Culture.* New York: Temple University Press; Joseph Foy and Stanley Schultz. (2009). *Homer Simpson Goes to Washington: American Politics through Popular Culture.* Lexington: The University Press of Kentucky; and Simon Frith. (2008). *Performing Rites: On the Value of Popular Music.* Cambridge, MA: Harvard University Press.
3. bell hooks. (1999). *Black Looks: Race and Representation.* South End Press.
4. Michele Foucault. (1980). *Power/Knowledge: Selected Interviews and Other Writings, 1972–1977.* New York: Vintage, p. 74.

FIFTEEN

Supervillains Who Need Superheroes (Are the Luckiest Villains in the World)

Andrew Smith

Andrew Smith is a nationally syndicated newspaper columnist who has, for decades, written an at least weekly column about comics and graphic novels. He was also is a contributing editor to the *Comics Buyer's Guide* for its last 13 years, and organizes the *Captain Comics Round Ttable website*, where he has his blog. His deep knowledge of superhero stories goes back to the 1960s, when he started collecting comics.

> I ask you to judge me by the enemies I have made.
> —Franklin D. Roosevelt

In the never-ending battle between superheroes and supervillains, most bad guys don't really care who rises to oppose them. They're in it for money, or world conquest, or any number of reasons that don't involve a recurring enemy. In fact, some villains are downright promiscuous in their sparring partners.

But a number of villains are very hero specific. They're usually referred to as archenemies or nemeses of their corresponding heroes, and they are usually mentioned in the same breath as their opponents (e.g., "Superman and Lex Luthor"). The motives and backgrounds of these characters vary, but what they have in common seems to be a need for an opposite number to complete or construct their own identity.

SUPERVILLAINS JUST WANT TO HAVE FUN

Some supervillains aren't interested in traditional villainy so much as they enjoy baiting or battling a given superhero. It's a game, a contest, or some other connection—one that sometimes borders on the intimate. We normally think of the word "intimate" as describing something affectionate or sexual, and in the case of some characters that is precisely true. But other emotions can bond characters intimately, like intense hatred, perverse pride, or manic fixation.

Take Dr. Doom, for example. His loathing of Reed Richards of the Fantastic Four is such that he probably knows more about Mr. Fantastic than Mrs. Richards does. Battling Richards is really his only joy.

In his 2004 "Fantastic Four Manifesto," *Fantastic Four* writer Mark Waid (2002–2004) called Doom "the most insecure man in the world." He "would tear the head off a newborn baby and eat it like an apple while his mother watched if it would somehow prove he were smarter than Reed."[1]

Another example is Flash's rogues gallery, a group of supervillains who plague the Scarlet Speedster so specifically that they are now called "Flash's Rogues" or, more simply, "The Rogues." The group formed in the 1960s and originally included Captain Boomerang, Captain Cold, Heat Wave, Mirror Master, Pied Piper, the Top, and Weather Wizard. Since then there have been a number of changes in the group's lineup, but what has been consistent is that they don't generally fight other superheroes, nor do they find some other, unprotected city where they could be successful crooks. In fact, they rarely appear anywhere but in the pages of *Flash*. It's telling that the group's name implies a connection to the Flash, and that they are annoyed when other villains horn in on their turf. They feel ownership over the Wizard of Whiz, and they take pride in their association with him and with one another. At times it almost seems like an exclusive social club—in fact, it's been established that no one can join the Rogues unless they all agree to it.

And for at least two female supervillains, battling their respective foes is tantamount to foreplay. Catwoman loves stealing for its own sake, certainly, but she also wants Batman to, um, "arrest" her—and the pair have been doing the horizontal "Batusi" for years.* At Marvel Comics, the Black Cat is a burglar with bad-luck powers who at one time committed crimes specifically to attract Spider-Man — and when she succeeded, they both "got lucky." In a titillating twist, Black Cat initially wanted Spidey to keep his mask on during sex, as she found Peter Parker boring.

Far less amusing is the Joker, who considers his lethal pranks a two-man game with Batman. After the Clown Prince of Crime had been missing from the pages of DC Comics for a few years, he was re-introduced in a 1973 story emphasizing his use of homicide to taunt the Dark Knight. At the climax, he tells Batman, "All the while I was behind bars, I *missed* our clashes! I *dreamed* of . . . *humiliating* you—in an especially *humorous* way!"[2] This idea has been present in every Joker story since.

Like the Rogues, the Joker has a sense of intimate ownership of his arch-foe. As Robert Greenberger writes in his Batman encyclopedia, "The Joker has considered Batman his personal property, actually interfering with the schemes of other felons if he felt it meant someone other than himself got to kill or unmask Batman."[3] For example, when the criminal kingpin Black Mask appears to have killed a Robin, the Joker assaults him, saying, "You took my job, stupid!. . . Oh, Blackie McMaskie, *everyone* knows my favorite job in the whole wide world is killing *Robin*!"[4]

MOM LIKED YOU BEST!

Some villains are insanely jealous of a specific superhero and direct all their malice at that specific character to prove their superiority. These characters feel their lives are incomplete, their successes meaningless, their lives hollow, unless the world acknowledges that the villain is the better man (or woman, or robot, or whatever). Two who epitomize that concept are Dr. Doom and Lex Luthor.

* Although sex between Batman and the Feline Fatale isn't new, the first issue of the new *Catwoman* title depicted the two writhing in half-dressed coitus, igniting a controversy among those who considered it too graphic. Judd Winick, ". . . and Most of the Costumes Stay On . . ." *Catwoman* #1, November 2011. New York: DC Comics, p. 20.

In a clear sign of petty jealousy, Victor von Doom constantly harps on the "inferior" intellectual capabilities and unwarranted public approval of his bête noir, Reed Richards of the Fantastic Four. Doom has on occasion made romantic plays for his enemy's wife, Sue "Invisible Woman" Richards—not because he actually desires her, but because he wants to possess what Richards has. (Doom isn't much of a romantic— he murdered his first and only girlfriend, sold her soul to demons, and made leather armor out of her skin.) When Sue miscarried the couple's second child, Doom saved both mother and daughter just to prove he could do what Richards couldn't—and then demanded the right to name the girl Valeria (after his dead girlfriend) so Richards would be reminded constantly of Doom's superiority.

In some ways, there seems to be something filial about Reed and Victor, even more so than between Richards and Ben "The Thing" Grimm, the latter an unrelated but de facto member of the Richards family. In fact, Doom seems like a twisted twin version of Richards, and their battles a kind of sibling rivalry.

Another example is Lex Luthor, who was Clark Kent's best childhood friend before becoming his worst enemy in at least three iterations: in comic books from the late 1950s to 1986, on the TV show *Smallville* (2001–2011), and in a short-lived comic book reboot (*Superman: Secret Origin*, 2009). In most versions of the Superman mythos, including the most recent re-launch in September 2011, Luthor doesn't meet Superman until both are adults, but there is still a sort of fratricidal vibe between the two. Mainly, Luthor is jealous of Superman's popularity in Metropolis, a city he regards as his personal fiefdom. As Greenberger says in his Superman encyclopedia, Luthor "grew to resent Superman for stealing the celebrity spotlight he had worked so hard to have all to himself."[5]

WHAT DOESN'T KILL ME...

For some villains, self-worth is tied up in the quality of their opponents. The greater the superheroes, the better the supervillains feel about themselves. By the same token, this type of villain seeks the hero's approval of the villain's schemes or acknowledgment of victory (and therefore superiority), often resulting in the much-mocked monologue.[*]

Luthor, for example, has fancied himself the hero who proves the superiority of human brain over alien brawn. In one of the earliest Superman-versus-Luthor battles (*Superman* #4, 1940), Luthor confidently challenges Superman to a contest: "If your muscles can surpass my scientific feats, I will admit defeat! But if I can outdo you, then you are to retire and leave me a clear path!"[6]

In the 1960s, Luthor's competition with the Man of Steel was even more pronounced. In an "Imaginary Story" in which Luthor manages to murder Superman, the former crows, "I've destroyed the mightiest man in the universe! What a glorious achievement!"[7] (And, yes, he monologues over the dying Superman.) Luthor's desire to

---

[*] One famous example of monologuing is found in the movie that first made the noun a verb, *The Incredibles* (2004). The villain Syndrome can't resist taunting Mr. Incredible with his grand scheme, despite the possibility that it will provide his foe with time to escape (which it does).

compete and win against Superman is such that when Luthor defeats Superman and robs Fort Knox, he ends up giving the gold back when he discovers it was just a Superman robot he conquered. "Even though I won a victory, I really lost!" he rants, throwing a gold bar (interestingly, at a statue of himself). "I didn't triumph over **Superman**, only a mechanical man! My sweet revenge has turned sour! All my work—all my plans—gone for nothing!"[8] Evidently, the gold he stole wasn't the point, as it would be for most crooks.

Even in the modern era, Luthor's preoccupation with Superman is apparent. When ensnared by Wonder Woman's lasso of truth, Luthor can't help saying, "What I really want...is to be Superman."[9] ("Of course you do," responds the Amazing Amazon.)

Magneto (real name Max Eisenhardt) is another character who would rather win the argument than the fight with Charles "Professor X" Xavier of the X-Men. When they first met in the newly formed Israel, Xavier and Eisenhardt (who was calling himself Erik Lensherr at the time) were allies, albeit ones who constantly argued. Xavier was a believer in peaceful coexistence between man and mutant, but Lensherr—a survivor of Nazi concentration camps—believed mutants' best hope for survival was either a separate country or mastery over humankind, and that violence was a perfectly acceptable way to achieve either.[10]

On at least two other occasions—on the devasted island of Genosha,* and earlier when Magneto acted as headmaster of the Xavier School for Gifted Youngsters—the two rekindled their friendship and managed to reconcile or look past their philosophical differences. But throughout, Eisenhardt has tried to prove to Xavier that mutants can't live with humans in harmony, while Professor X has argued the reverse. Both would rather convince the other than kill him.

THIS IS ALL YOUR FAULT!

For many arch-villains, a hero is someone onto whom they can project their failures or who can be used as an excuse for less-than-meritorious actions. In the 1989 *Batman* movie, the Joker says, "You made me. Remember? You dropped me into a vat of chemicals," referring to his own origin in which he fell into that vat to escape Batman's pursuit. Despite the obvious truth that it was the Joker's own actions that put him in the Axis Chemical Company and his own clumsiness that caused the fall, he puts the blame on Batman.

This isn't the only origin for the Joker,† but in virtually all scenarios, Batman remains the Joker's motivational force and, in recent years, a homoerotic fixation. Both are demonstrated perfectly in the possible future of *Batman: The Dark Knight Returns*: the Joker goes catatonic when Batman retires, and doesn't move again until

---

* In the Marvel Universe, Genosha was an island off the east coast of Africa that the United Nations ceded to Magneto as a mutant nation. It was destroyed by an army of Sentinels, giant mutant-hunting robots, in an attack that killed 16 million mutants and humans.

† The chemical-vat origin for the Joker is mirrored in at least one comic book story, Bill Finger's "The Man Behind the Red Hood" (*Detective Comics* #168, February 1951). But there have been other origins as well. As explained by the Joker himself in Alan Moore's 1988 graphic novel *Batman: The Killing Joke*, "If I'm going to have a past, I prefer it to be multiple choice!" (p. 39).

he sees the Caped Crusader on TV, saying as he awakens, "BB...BBBat...Batman. Darling."[11] Ever since that 1986 story, the Joker has shown a marked preference for terms of endearment when referring to the Dark Knight.

CONCLUSION

As Franklin Roosevelt suggested, some want to be judged by whom they fight. Some villains need their opposites to define themselves, even if only in opposition. Perhaps they secretly fear that they are only reflections or shadows of heroes, without whom they would have little reason to exist.

One Joker story captures my argument best. In "Emperor Joker," a story that ran through a number of Superman books for several months, the Joker gains magical powers and can change the world at will. But Superman beats the Clown Prince of Crime by challenging him to kill Batman once and for all. Try as he might, and even with godlike powers, the Joker will not—or cannot—do it. Superman has identified the Joker's psychological Achilles heel: he desperately needs Batman as a reason to exist.

"Your universe can't have **meaning**...without a **Batman**,"[12] says the Man of Steel. The Joker might be crazy, but even he can't deny that hard truth.

NOTES

1. Mark Waid. (2004). *Fantastic Four,* Vol. 1. New York: Marvel Comics.
2. Denny O'Neil, "The Joker's Five-Way Revenge!" *Batman* #251, September 1973. New York: DC Comics, p. 14.
3. Robert Greenberger. (2008). *The Essential Batman Encyclopedia.* New York: Ballantine Books, p. 195.
4. Andersen Gabrych, "War Crimes Part 3: A Consequence of Truth," *Detective Comics* #810, October 2005. New York: DC Comics, p. 22.
5. Robert Greenberg and Martin Pasko. (2010). *The Essential Superman Encyclopedia.* New York: Ballantine Books, p. 222.
6. Jerry Siegel, "The Challenge of Luthor!" *Superman* #4, Spring 1940. New York: DC Comics, p. 5. This story was unnamed when first published, but *Superman Chronicles Volume Three* (New York: DC Comics, 2007) has retroactively assigned a title.
7. Jerry Siegel, "The Death of Superman!" *Superman* #149, November 1961. New York: DC Comics, p. 16.
8. Bill Finger, "The Conquest of Superman!" *Action Comics* #277, June 1961. New York: DC Comics, p. 11.
9. Geoff Johns, "Blackest Night Part Seven," *Blackest Night* #7, April 2010. New York: DC Comics, p. 17.
10. Chris Claremont, "Gold Rush!" *Uncanny X-Men* #161, September 1982. New York: Marvel Comics, pp. 1–21.
11. Frank Miller. (1986). "The Dark Knight Returns." *Batman: The Dark Knight Returns Book One.* New York: DC Comics, p. 33.
12. Joe Kelly, "He Who Laughs Last," *Action Comics* #770, October 770. New York: DC Comics, p. 22.

SIXTEEN

Sorting Out Villainy: A Typology of Villains and Their Effects on Superheroes

Robin S. Rosenberg

Robin S. Rosenberg is a clinical psychologist; she writes about superheroes and the psychological phenomena their stories reveal. She is author of *Superhero Origins: What Makes Superheroes Tick and Why We Care*, and *What's the Matter With Batman? An Unauthorized Clinical Look Under the Mask of the Caped Crusader* as well as college-level psychology textbooks. She is editor of *Psychology of Superheroes* and *Our Superheroes, Ourselves* and editor of the *Superhero* series by Oxford University Press; she is also co-editor of this volume.

Supervillains are important inhabitants of the world of superheroes. Villains are drawn to crime—and different types of crime—for a variety of reasons. Some are simply greedy. Some are vengeful, selfish, psychopaths, or mentally disturbed in other ways. Some see themselves in the role of the hero on a mission that requires moral flexibility. Still others are sadists, causing harm for the thrill of it. Some villains are driven by a combination of these motivations.

These motivations mean that superheroes battle different types of villains, and each type of villain elicits a different challenge for superheroes and creates different types of stories. Each type of villain creates different "lessons," for both superheroes and readers or viewers, and reveals different aspects of the superheroes' mettle.

I've created a typology of villains based on their motives and actions. In what follows, I discuss how the different types of villains engage and reveal different facets of superheroes. This typology is loosely derived from the typology of evil proposed by psychologist Roy Baumeister in his book *Evil: Inside Human Violence and Cruelty*.*

THE STRAIGHTFORWARD CRIMINAL

The *straightforward criminal* seeks either material gain—in money or valuable objects—or power and acts illegally to get it. This type of villain isn't generally "super" and so provides less of a challenge for the superhero, and consequently less interesting stories. Many of the early superhero stories typically involved this type of villain (such as Alex Greer, the crooked lobbyist from *Action Comics* #1, or Alfred Stryker, the criminal at the head of the chemical syndicate from *Detective Comics* #27). Modern incarnations include Marvel's Kingpin, who is motivated to acquire money and power; Batman's villain, the Penguin (in comic book stories); and Catwoman, who in many stories is motivated to acquire feline-themed objects. Straightforward criminals want "more"

---

* To anyone interested in the whats, whys, and hows of evil and its psychological underpinnings, I heartily recommend this book, published in 1996 by W. H. Freeman and Co.

of their hearts' desires and engage in criminal acts to get it. They generally don't harm or kill people unless they must, either to obtain their desired object or to display their power strategically. Their illegal acts are the means to their ends.

Such villains allow the superhero to fight openly for justice and the rule of law, and often these stories portray relatively clear-cut cases of right versus wrong. Stories with these villains may show superheroes as superpowered extensions of law enforcement.

THE VENGEFUL VILLAIN

A more interesting type of villain—both in terms of the story and for what he or she elicits in the superhero—is the *vengeful villain*: the thwarted criminal whose actions stem from a personal vendetta. Typically, this type of villain has it out for the superhero. The villain's conflict with the superhero is personal. This type of villain's crimes and shenanigans are motivated not simply by greed—though that may be a part of it—but by revenge. The vengeful villain wants either to eliminate the superhero or to prove him- or herself superior to the superhero. The villain typically seeks not simply to kill or beat but to outsmart, outfight, or humiliate the superhero. At his or her most extreme, the villain is only satisfied with beating the superhero where the superhero is strongest, to prove superiority in every way and seek retribution for whatever "injury" the villain perceives himself or herself to have previously sustained from the superhero. In fact, it is hurt pride that leads vengeful villains to inflict disproportionate "harm" to the superhero.[1] It's a never-ending contest. From the superhero's perspective, the conflicts take the form of battles of wits or brawn, and the villain must be apprehended and locked up. Such battles can be a burdensome duty for the superhero, particularly when the intensity of the villain's malevolence ratchets up over time. The superhero might wish he or she didn't have to engage in these battles but is resigned to them like some kind of repetitive chore. Examples include Reed Richards's skirmishes with Dr. Doom and Superman's with Lex Luthor.

Lex Luthor, Superman's arch-nemesis, provides possibly the best example of the vengeful villain. In one version of Luthor's origin, he and young Clark Kent are teen-age friends in Smallville. Luthor is a scientist even then, and a fire in his lab gets out of control. Superboy, using his superbreath, tames the fire but inadvertently creates a combination of fumes that cause Luthor's hair to fall out. Rather than thank Superboy for saving his life, Luthor attributes hostile motives to Superboy's actions and blames Superboy for what becomes Luthor's permanent baldness. Luthor vows revenge. "My arch-enemy, Luthor, might have been the world's greatest benefactor!" sighed Superman aloud in November 1962. "But he lost his hair in an accidental explosion and blamed me for his baldness! In his bitterness he became Earth's most evil criminal scientist!" (*Adventure Comics* #271, 1960).

As vengeful villains seek revenge, they look for the chink in the superhero's armor. It is often these stories that allow us to see the superhero not only as a hero with powers, but as someone vulnerable and more like us. The villains typically do find some flaw. They figure out who the superhero cares about and kidnap that person. Examples abound. The Fantastic Four's Sue or Johnny Storm gets trapped in another dimension as a way to get at Reed Richards. Mary Jane is kidnapped surprisingly frequently just to make Spider-Man squirm. Some vengeful villains learn that kidnapping is not enough. They go one step further and make superheroes choose between saving their loved one or many innocent people. This forced choice is a staple of many superhero stories, and a notable example is found in the film *Spider-Man* (2002), in which the Green Goblin kidnaps Mary Jane to compel Spider-Man to face one of the most difficult choices known to humankind.

Some straightforward criminals can become vengeful villains after the superhero thwarts their plans. Luthor traveled this exact path. In *Action Comics* #23 (1940), Superman demolishes Luthor's floating fortress and wrecks the human's plans to make himself "supreme master of the world." After a series of confrontations, Luthor is able (temporarily) to gain powers greater than Superman's, and instead of using that power to accomplish his goals, he spends the whole story trying to defeat and humiliate Superman. Another example of the path from straightforward criminal to vengeful villain is found in the film *Spider-Man* (2002): The villain Green Goblin shifts to being a vengeful villain after Spider-Man turns down Goblin's offer for them to be partners in crime. This rejection spurs the Green Goblin to seek revenge on Spider-Man. Just as in our world we can inadvertently create our own enemies through our actions, so too with superheroes.

THE HEROIC VILLAIN

A third type of supervillain can be thought of as a "heroic" villain in that this type of villain has an "altruistic" cause and an ultimate goal that is more than acquiring money or jewels. The heroic villain believes that he or she is working for some greater good. This type of villain sees himself or herself as a hero, and the superhero as someone who thwarts the villain's worthwhile actions and goals. He or she has a goal that isn't selfish, although it might be a bit twisted. Like superheroes, then, heroic villains fight for a cause. From their point of view, they are heroes, and their ends justify their destructive means.

A few examples of this type of villain stand out, with perhaps the best one being Batman's nemesis Poison Ivy, who is considered to be an eco-terrorist. She is passionate about the primacy of plant life over human life and sees herself as a defender of the weak and oppressed (namely, plants), which she sees as her children.* When she harms humans, she feels she is punishing those who deserve it, just as superheroes apprehend villains who deserve to be put away. As she says in an episode of *Gotham Girls*,[2] "I'm an eco-terrorist of global importance. I make a contribution."

Another example of a heroic villain is the X-Men's sometimes-nemesis Magneto, who uses his powers not for traditionally selfish reasons, but for the betterment of mutantkind, so that mutants can get the same (and perhaps more) rights as regular humans. Should humans be hurt in the process, it's not his concern.

---

* Although there is something personal between Ivy and Batman, in that he is one of the few people who are able to foil her plans, her actions aren't motivated primarily by revenge.

The third example of the heroic villain is Batman's enemy Ra's al-Ghul, who seeks to make a more stable and thus "better" world. Unfortunately, his mechanism for doing so invariably involves some form of mass murder or other harming of innocents. Another heroic villain with a similar general goal and means to an end is Ozymandias from *Watchmen*,[3] who kills millions of innocent victims in a faked alien incursion in order to unite the United States and the Soviet Union against a common enemy and thus prevent the mutually assured nuclear destruction the two countries are heading toward. Note that the line between heroic villain and anti-hero (such as the Punisher, a vigilante who wages war against criminals) can be fuzzy and depends in part on the point of view from which the story is told.

Because heroic villains believe they fight for right, they are different from other types of villains who recognize that their actions are illegal or immoral and thus "wrong." The heroic supervillains believe their goals and actions are set on a higher moral plane. Because they don't see themselves as doing anything wrong, and in fact see themselves as doing "good," their actions prompt the superhero to wrestle with his or her own moral conscience about what is right and wrong. Heroic villains are fighting to right a perceived injustice or to make the world, in their view, a better place. In this way, they aren't so dissimilar from superheroes; it's just that the specifics are different regarding what constitutes an injustice, what the "better place" would look like, for whom it would be better, and at what cost.

THE SADISTIC SUPERVILLAIN

Perhaps no other type of villain is as frightening as the sadistic supervillain—the type who wreaks havoc simply because he or she can and who enjoys it. This pleasure is the main motive. Sadistic supervillains leave trails of death and destruction to get their kicks. The Joker exemplifies the sadistic supervillain, and the best example of this aspect of his character is in the film *The Dark Knight*. This Joker is a self-appointed "agent of chaos" who clearly enjoys frightening and hurting others for the fun of it. His twisted sense of humor is evident in the forced-choice, life-and-death dilemma the Joker sets up with two ships, giving passengers on each ship the power to kill everyone on board the other ship and informing them that a ticking bomb will sink both ships if neither ship acts to destroy the other. The Joker creates this horrific dilemma for the fun of watching what will happen. As the Joker says to Batman in *The Dark Knight*, "I won't kill you because you're too much fun." Similarly, in some stories, Loki, Thor's brother, refuses to kill the thunder god so that he can go on tormenting him.

The traits of the sadistic supervillain are best described in this quote from the film *The Dark Knight*, in which the Joker taunts a detective assigned as his guard at the stationhouse: "Do you want to know why I use a knife? Guns are too quick. You can't savor all the…little emotions. In…you see, in their last moments, people show you who they really are. So in a way, I know your friends better than you ever did. Would you like to know which of them were cowards?"

Sadistic villains may share some outward traits with vengeful villains; they might kidnap the superhero's loved one and force the superhero to choose between saving the loved one or a group of innocents. The kidnapping might even have a personal element, as it does with vengeful villains. The difference is that sadistic villains also are motivated by the pain of the innocents, not just that of the superhero.

Stories with sadistic supervillains show us what the superhero is made of because the superhero must come face to face with evil. Battling the sadistic supervillain is like battling pure evil. There seems to be no end to the bad things this villain can make happen, no depths to which he or she won't make others sink. The superhero must witness all of the sadistic villain's horrific actions, which can wear down most superheroes.

It's not simply the battles that wear down the superhero. To prevent future crimes by this type of villain, superheroes often try to get into the minds of their foes, to think like the villains in order to predict their actions. But getting inside the mind of a sadistic supervillain is dirty work and can leave the superhero feeling tainted; it can twist the superhero's notions of right and wrong as the superhero fights "dirty" to apprehend the sadistic villain. For instance, in the film *The Dark Knight*, Batman has to start thinking like the Joker, even fighting very dirty like the Joker (such as by crossing an ethical line and turning every cell phone in Gotham City into a surveillance device).

DC's major superheroes are similarly forced to wrestle with their consciences and behave in an "amoral" way when the wife of a Justice League member is killed and it seems that their enemy Dr. Light will kill other loved ones.[4] To protect their loved ones, the superheroes decide essentially to lobotomize Dr. Light. These types of moral choices that the superheroes must make rarely occur when the villain is motivated by anything other than the "sport" of blood and emotional pain.

Stories with sadist villains thus induce the superhero to wrestle with his or her conscience about what can be sacrificed for the greater good, about whether it is possible to stay on the side of "right" when fighting someone who is so "wrong." Such stories invoke existential dilemmas for the superheroes that we can relate to as we try to grapple with the "evil" in our world and understand why some people commit horrific and destructive acts.

THE SUPERVILLAIN SHAPES THE SUPERHERO

Villains aren't a monolithic group. They're motivated by different forces, they desire different goals, they use different means. Villains come in different types, each of which induce different emotions, thoughts, and struggles for the superhero. Each type of villain, then, reveals a different aspect of the superhero. In doing so, each aspect that comes to the fore provides an added dimension to the definition of the superhero.

NOTES

1. Roy F. Baumeister. (1996). *Evil: Inside Human Cruelty and Violence*. New York: W. H. Freeman.
2. (2001). "Scout's Dis-Honor" [Television series episode]. In A. Bruckner (Producer), *Gotham Girls*. Warner Brothers & Noodle Soup.
3. Alan Moore and Dave Gibbons. (1986). *The Watchmen*. New York: DC Comics.
4. Brad Meltzer and Rags Morales. (2004). *Identity Crisis*. New York: DC Comics.

From the Experts: Comic Book Writers Define the Superhero

No book that explores the definition of a superhero can be considered complete without the opinions of the people who create superheroes and their stories. After all, it is such professionals who provide the materials from which scholars and fans cull their own definitions. It is these professionals who have created and who expand the definition, the context, and the genre of superheroes. Through the essays in this section, we learn how superhero writers and creators define superheroes for themselves, how they think about the roles of context, costume, and culture, and how superheroes are shaped by their supervillains.

SEVENTEEN

More Than Normal, But Believable

Stan Lee

Stan Lee's name is practically synonymous with the word "superhero." He co-created many famous superheroes during his time at Marvel Comics: the Incredible Hulk, the Fantastic Four, Thor, Spider-Man, Iron Man, and the X-Men, among many others. Stan imbued his characters and stories with an element of psychological realism, making it easy for fans to relate to the characters and their plights. Stan became an editor at Marvel when he was 19 years old and went on to become its publisher. Stan continues to create new superheroes under the banner of his *POW! Entertainment* company.

A superhero is *a person who does heroic deeds and has the ability to do them in a way that a normal person couldn't.* So in order to be a superhero, you need a power that is more exceptional than any power a normal human being could possess, and you need to use that power to accomplish good deeds. Otherwise, a policeman or a fireman could be considered a superhero. For instance, a good guy fighting a bad guy could be just a regular police story or detective story or human-interest story. But if it's a good guy with a superpower who is fighting a bad guy, it becomes a superhero story. If the good guy is doing something that a normal human being couldn't do, couldn't accomplish, then I assume he becomes a superhero.

Not surprisingly, then, the first thing I would think of when trying to create a character is, what superpower will I give him or her? I'll make somebody who can throw fireballs and fly in the air. I'll have somebody who can crawl on walls and shoot webs like a spider. So, automatically, those characters become superheroes. Of course, if they were evil, they would be supervillains, because the same rule applies: to be a supervillain, you have to be a villain, but you also have to have a superpower, just like a superhero has to. The word *super* is really the key.

But there's no formula for creating characters. With Iron Man, I knew I wanted someone in an iron suit, and so his powers came from that. With Spider-Man, I knew I wanted someone with spider powers, so the name and costume came with that. It doesn't matter whether you start with the character's code name, his powers, or his costume; none of these conventions of the genre works better than the others as a starting place for creating a superhero. It just depends on whether you get lucky and what sells.

There doesn't necessarily have to be a connection between the personality of the alter ego and the powers of the superhero. When we created the Fantastic Four, I knew that I wanted each of them to have distinct powers. Even though Reed is mentally bright and flexible, Johnny is a bit of a hothead, Sue is a shrinking violet, and Ben is a big lug—which fits with their powers—I could have made Sue go on and on and speak with big words, or made Johnny the intellectual, or given Reed a temper. The powers of the characters don't necessarily have to reflect the personalities of the characters, and the Fantastic Four would have been just as successful if there had been no link between their personalities and their powers. It just depends on how it works out. That's the way things were back then.

The problem with telling superhero stories is that it naturally follows that you need a supervillain. You need a foe who can make the story interesting, someone who's at least as powerful as—and hopefully even more powerful than—the hero, because that makes the story fun. The viewer or the reader has to think to himself or herself, how is our hero ever going to get out of this? How is he ever going to beat the villain? We have to keep the reader on the edge of his or her seat. So the most important thing is to have a supervillain who is equally as colorful as and even more powerful than the hero apparently is.

I try to make the characters seem as believable and realistic as possible. In order to do that, I have to place them in the real world, or, if the story is set in an imaginary world, I have to try to make that imaginary world as realistic-seeming as possible, so the character doesn't exist in a vacuum. He has to have friends, enemies, people he's in love with, people he doesn't love—just like any human being. I try to take the super-hero and put him in as normal a world as possible, and the contrast between him and his power and the normal world is one of the things that make the stories colorful and believable and interesting.

Superman was the start of the whole superhero thing. He had the superpowers and wore that costume with the bright colors and silly cape. It's the costume that was different. Zorro didn't have superpowers, Doc Savage* didn't have superpowers; they could just do things a little better than the rest of us. The Shadow† could be a superhero because he could make himself unseen, and if he appeared in a comic book today, he might be a superhero, though he doesn't really wear a costume. I'm not an expert on the Shadow, but I think he just had a dark business suit and a sort of raincoat and a slouch hat. Superman's costume was different because of the bright colors, that silly cape, those red boots, his belt, and his chest symbol. I mean, it's ridiculous, because you really don't need a costume to fly or fight bad guys. If I had superpowers, I wouldn't wear a costume. But it does serve as a way of colorfully identifying the superhero, and it also announces him. When he gets into a fight with a bad guy, the costume sort of explains that he's the good guy.

Although a costume isn't required of superheroes, the fans love costumes. The characters are more popular if they wear costumes. (Don't ask me why.) In the first issue of the Fantastic Four, I didn't have them wear costumes. I received a ton of

---

* Editors' note: Doc Savage is Clark Savage, Jr., a pulp adventurer whose adventures were published by Street and Smith from 1933 to 1949 and who has seen numerous paperback and comic book revivals. He is also the subject of a campy 1975 feature film, *Doc Savage: The Man of Bronze*, starring Ron Ely.

† The Shadow is a dark pulp vigilante who debuted in 1931 and went on to be the subject of a radio series, movie serials, paperbacks, comics, and a feature film. On radio he was voiced by Orson Welles and other actors, and he was played by Alec Baldwin in the 1994 film. He is often depicted as having the power to "cloud men's minds" in order to be invisible. Writer Bill Finger was influenced by the depiction of the Shadow when he co-created Batman.

mail from fans saying that they loved the book, but they wouldn't buy another issue unless we gave the characters costumes. I didn't need a house to fall on me to realize that—for whatever reason—fans love costumed heroes.

I think people are fascinated by superheroes because when we were young we all liked fairy tales, and fairy tales are stories of people with superpowers, people who are super in some way—giants, witches, magicians, always people who are bigger than life. Well, as we got older, we outgrew fairy tales. Most people don't read fairy tales when they're grown-ups, but I don't think we ever outgrow our love for those kinds of stories, stories of people who are bigger and more powerful and more colorful than we are. So superhero stories, to me, are like fairy tales for grown-ups. I don't know why, but the human condition is such that we love reading about people who can do things that we can't do and who have powers that we wish we had.

EIGHTEEN

Making the World a Better Place

Jeph Loeb

Jeph Loeb is an Emmy Award–nominated and Eisner Award–winning writer/producer. His many credits include *Heroes*, *Lost*, and *Smallville* in television and *Teen Wolf* and *Commando* in film. Jeph has written nearly every major comics icon, including the Avengers, Hulk, Iron Man, Spider-Man, Wolverine, Batman, and Superman.

The easy answer to the question of "What is a superhero?" is that superheroes are people with powers and abilities beyond those of mortal men. But the more difficult answer is that they are people with such powers and abilities who make a choice to use them to help those who need it; using their gifts in this way is a selfless act intended to make a better world. Superheroes do this in different ways: Batman does it through fear and intimidation, the Punisher does it with a rifle, Spider-Man does it with humor, the Hulk does it through smashing, and Superman and Captain America do it through inspiring us to be the best that we can be.

There isn't a wrong way to portray a superhero working to make the world a better place, but there needs to be a commitment that drives the drama of the story. What makes it inspirational is that we all at some point in our lives face what we would consider insurmountable odds, whether it's standing on a baseball mound or paying a bill without enough funds to cover the payment. It's at those times that we have to reach inside of ourselves to push on. In the real world, the heroes are the teachers and the doctors, and other people who give their time to the less fortunate. Those are the people who superhero stories are based on, and those are the stories that inspire us to become people who help others, because as fun and dramatic as it would be to put on a cape and jump out of the window, in the real world it would make for a very short career.

So if you want to live in the real world and see the inherent value of what these people do, you have to look toward occupations and volunteering that enable you to help others. Now, some would argue that the work of those of us who are lucky enough to work in the storytelling profession is heroic. It could be said that by telling the stories of the heroes in comic books, movies, television, and animation, we are doing a heroic act. I can only hope these stories brighten somebody else's day, so that maybe in that small way their telling becomes a heroic act. It's difficult for me to see that in myself, because I enjoy what I do.

Superheroes inspire people. I know this to be true because of the people I meet at comic book conventions and people who comment online. People take lessons from superhero characters and stories: "Well, if Peter Parker can get through that, then I can get through this." Character identification runs throughout all of literature, not just pop culture. Movies that really connect with people do so on a very human level—people see something of themselves in these heroes, and they see the choice between good and evil. Any depiction of good triumphing over evil, I believe, betters the world because it gives folks, particularly children, a vision of right and wrong that they might not be getting in other ways. I don't believe that if I simply show a kid a story about Captain America or Thor he or she will automatically turn out to be a "good guy" any more than I believe that if a child plays *Grand Theft Auto* he or she will turn into a car thief. There are a lot of other social and societal elements that go in to the final mix. But it can't hurt!

The moral stories we tell are very much biblical in nature, in the sense that there are consequences to the characters' actions: you don't get to take a shortcut without finding shortcomings. These are moral lessons, and the best comics are ones that try to inspire (I don't think *teach* is the right word). You get something from stories, whether they're told in comics or on *Buffy the Vampire Slayer*, *Smallville*, or even *Lost*. Hopefully, they are stories of redemption and stories of inspiration. The stories create real-world problems around fantastical situations.

That's the fun of *Smallville*: in the beginning, the villains were the head coach, a tyrannical hothead who would burst into flames, or the ice princess who could actually freeze people. The worst aspect of your personality would become the power that you manifested after exposure to kryptonite. You saw how erratic the lives of the people who developed powers became because they didn't have the moral compass Clark did with his parents, Jonathan and Martha Kent. Clark's life inevitably turned out better because he had his adoptive parents to guide him. Clark's integrity couldn't come without a price, though: he couldn't be honest with his friends, and certainly at the beginning of the series his love for Lana went unrequited.*

Any story that I work on begins with a protagonist, and I ask myself very simple questions: what does this person want, what is keeping him or her from achieving that goal, and does the person achieve that goal? It's very simple—a sort of Storytelling 101. Cinderella is a great example that I use when I teach. What does Cinderella want? To go to the ball and meet the handsome prince. What prevents that from happening? She's impoverished, and she's got wicked stepsisters and a wicked stepmother who are the villains of the piece. In the end, though, she succeeds and meets the handsome prince. Her success doesn't come without complications—the clock strikes midnight and she turns back into her old self—yet in the end she still succeeds.

I divide things up between the plot and the story, a practice I credit to Mike Nichols. I read that Mike Nichols once said that the difference between the plot and the story was that in the plot, the queen died and then the king died. In the story, the queen died, and then the king died of a broken heart. You can see that there's a difference, because you've now inserted a human element into that story. In the story of Cinderella, if you ask people what Cinderella wants, they'll tell you that she wants to go to the ball and meet the handsome prince. That might be what Cinderella wants in the plot, but that's not what Cinderella wants in the story. What Cinderella wants

---

* Editors' note: Lana Lang is a character in Superman comics, films, and television shows; Clark Kent went to high school with her, and she was his first love.

in the story is to be loved for who she is. So she believes, erroneously, that if her fairy godmother puts her in a beautiful gown and gives her glass slippers, she will then be able to win the love of the handsome prince, because she will have become another person. The real resonance of that story is that the handsome prince comes to find her, and when he finds her, she is impoverished again. She is who she is. She is Cinderella. She is not a princess; she is back inside this horrible life she lives, and yet the prince sees through all of that and still loves her. In the end, she gets what she wants. She gets the handsome prince, she gets loved, and at the same time, depending on how the story is told, she gets to live in the castle.

So, any story—whether it's about Bruce Banner or the Hulk, Peter Parker or Spider-Man—is about what the protagonist wants. What's the goal? And if all you have for the story is that he wants to make sure that Doc Ock* doesn't blow up the world, then you don't really have much of a story. If you insert into that story details like that what Spider-Man really wants is to make sure that he gets back by 5:00 p.m. because he's promised Mary Jane that he's going to take her out to dinner, and that the reason he doesn't want Doc Ock to blow up the world is that he loves his Aunt May and wants to protect the world to make sure that she's O.K., now you've got a reality in that story that people can understand.

Joe Quesada† tells a story about how when he was first working on *Daredevil*, he went to go see Stan Lee, who created Daredevil, and said, "Stan, what's the secret?" And I'm going to tell this story badly, because I'm not Stan Lee. But according to the legend, Stan said, "Well, if you start with a man in a red suit who is standing on a ledge on a 50-story building, it's interesting. You don't see that every day. You sort of seriously wonder what the man is doing in a red suit on a 50-story building. But you're then told that the man is blind, and that he's a lawyer who fights against injustice, and that he has been blind since he was a child because he pushed a man he didn't even know out of the way of an oncoming truck and sacrificed his sight. And then you find out that the reason he's that way is that his father was a heavyweight prize fighter who, because he loved his son so much, refused to take a dive when the mob was trying to get their hooks into him. That man up there on that ledge, on that 50-story building in that red suit, we now have a vested interest in what's going to happen to him. That's the most important part of telling a story."

It really isn't about the powers, the abilities, or whoever the superhero is going to punch. The story is about the people. That's why an argument could be made that Peter Parker, Matt Murdoch, and Bruce Banner are infinitely more interesting than their respective superhero counterparts of Spider-Man, the Hulk, and Daredevil simply because they're real people in an extraordinary situation.

The costume is a challenging aspect of superhero stories. I completely understand that Bruce Wayne's life was destroyed because he witnessed the murder of his parents, and I completely understand someone who grows up, trains himself, and makes

---

* Editors' note: Doc Ock (short for Doctor Octopus) is a Spider-Man villain.
† Editors' note: See Joe Quesada's essay in this volume for a similar story that Stan Lee told Joe Quesada at another point in time.

a promise on the grave of his parents to rid the city of the evil that took their lives. The part that requires a leap of faith is that he's going to do that while he's dressed in his pajamas. And for good or for bad, that is something that comes with the superhero genre. It is always difficult to make a uniform work. It is one of the things that, for whatever reason, tend to work a little better over on the Marvel side of things, partially because when you look at Iron Man, it seems plausible that you could get inside his teched-out suit of armor. It seems plausible that you could become a giant green monster after gamma exposure or a shot in the arm. The story of Dr. Jekyll and Mr. Hyde doesn't require anyone putting on a cape. So, adding the costume to represent the other identity creates a different way of looking at things.

That said, the costume is important as a visual icon of the character's mission and identity. Batman became a bat because he thought that it would instill fear into criminals, who are a cowardly and superstitious lot. So he would become the bat, a thing of the night that would scare them.

But the costume can also embody the evolution of a character. Superman's costume is very much a testament to his identity, or, rather, identities. For a long, long time, the "S" symbol on his costume just stood for "Superman." But a major shift took place in the film *Superman* in 1978. The start of the movie reveals the "S" symbol as the crest of the House of El; it's worn by his father Jor-El before the destruction of Krypton. On Earth, Lois Lane is the first to refer to the unnamed superhero as "Superman" in the article she publishes after interviewing him. So within the world of the story, the "S" symbol honors Superman's Kryptonian heritage, and then it's customized by a reporter for a great metropolitan newspaper who sees it as signifying his superhero persona. Thus the symbol comes to represents both his Kal-El and his Superman identities.

I did something similar with Daredevil's costume in *Daredevil: Yellow*. Daredevil's original costume was yellow, and then it became red in the seventh issue of the series without any explanation. It simply happened between Issues 6 and 7, and there isn't even a blurb on the cover announcing the new costume. The origin and meaning of the costume weren't important when superheroes were created back then; no one really dug that deeply into the meaning of the costume. In retelling the early story of Daredevil in the present day, I wanted the costume and the change in its color to have some kind of underpinning that could come from some place of meaning. I want the costumes that superheroes wear to be emblems of the things that they believe in.

In this particular case, Daredevil's origin is a father-and-son story. "Battling" Jack Murdoch was part of the reason that his son Matt could fight, but fighting was the very thing that Matt's father hoped he would not do. This tension prompted Matt to split himself into two people: Daredevil and Matt Murdoch. Matt Murdoch became the person that his father wanted him to be, a lawyer. Then Daredevil became the person that Matt wanted to be, a fighter. His father was a boxer, and he very much wanted to be like his father, who was the biggest hero of his life. It is not unusual for a person to be inspired by his or her parents and want to honor them, and that's where I decided the original costume came from: Matt made it out of his father's yellow boxing robe as part of creating a new identity so that he could seek justice for his father, who was murdered by gangsters for refusing to throw a fight. Once Matt put the gangsters away, his costume changed to red, but no one ever explained why. The color change was a very simple thing: red was the favorite color of Karen Page, Matt's girlfriend, and because *Daredevil* is also a love story, the new costume design was something that he got from her. And that really became the transition in the story—he had honored his father, had gotten justice for his father's murder, and had become a man on his own. He would always remember his father and love his father, but it was time for him to move on to the next part in his life, and in doing so, he embraced a new costume and the woman whom he loved. In this storyline, the change of costume, which was never explained, now starts to make sense in an emotional way for the character.

We live in a very complicated world. As much as we find ourselves immersed in the Internet and in the world of Twitter, there's an immediacy to our lives that we've never known before—almost instant knowledge, instant reactions. Before you're even done seeing the movie that you're seeing, someone's posted a review. Before you've even gone on a date, 11 of your Facebook friends have commented on the person that you are thinking about going out with. The time needed to think about the human condition is often slipping away. What superhero stories do, when they're told well, is make us slow down and think about the situations that we're in and the people that we're affecting—at least, the best stories do. This is why, more than ever, it's a time for heroes. If we take that pause and really look at our lives and seek to be both inspired and inspirational—and a little less self-absorbed—we can make the world a much better place than it currently is. At least, I hope we can.

NINETEEN

Power and Responsibility…and Other Reflections on Superheroes

Danny Fingeroth

Danny Fingeroth is probably best known for his time at Marvel Comics as the Spider-Man group editor, but he has been recognized as a leading commentator about superheroes and comics. He has written two books analyzing superheroes: *Superman On The Couch: What Superheroes Really Tell Us About Ourselves and Our Society* and *Disguised as Clark Kent: Jews, Comics and the Creation of the Superhero*. He is the co-editor (with Roy Thomas) of *The Stan Lee Universe*.

Every superhero has as his or her basis the Spider-Man credo: "With great power, there must also come—great responsibility." Stan Lee, who penned this motto in Spider-Man's debut story in 1962's *Amazing Fantasy* #15, was the first to spell that philosophy out in a manner at once so elegant and direct. Someone has or obtains enhanced power—physical, mental, magical, mechanical—and then, either through good character or a difficult, transformative rite of passage, realizes that power confers on them an obligation to some section of humanity, if not all of it. Superheroes and their powers are central metaphors for growing up, from child to adolescent and adolescent to adult.

In keeping with the power/responsibility equation, it follows that a superhero is a figure who embodies the best aspects of humankind, differing from a heroic real person or even a fictional non-super hero due to—in addition to one or more special powers or mechanical or magical enhancements—a nobility of purpose, which is what makes him or her not a super*villain*. Supervillains may also believe themselves to have a noble purpose or special mission—indeed, the best supervillains do—but, at the very least, their *means* toward their ends are negative.

The superhero's ultimate mission is to defend the defenseless and give strength to the powerless. If we're all somehow "the little guy," then the superhero is fighting the good fight for us. This is true both when they are having problems in their personal lives and when they are battling cosmic menaces. At their best, superhero stories can do what all great literature does—tell us something about the human condition in a way that we may not have thought about before. I like to think I've written and edited some stories that inspired someone somewhere to face down his or her own supervillains, inner or outer.

The closer the superhero's mission of the moment impacts on, or is impacted by, his or her personal life and problems, the more satisfying the story will be. The risk with this approach to a story is that a given hero can be seen as self-involved in a way that dilutes the nobility of purpose—his or her mission of doing good for the people the hero is obligated to protect. Done well, though, it can enhance that nobility.

The conflicts and challenges that the superhero faces must be larger than life, while still mirroring readers' real concerns. Aside from the use of superpowers and /or advanced technology, which of course are clear indicators of a superhero tale, such a story is marked, paradoxically, by a certain down-to-earth quality which tells us that, despite the trappings of outlandish costumes and over-the-top language, the people we are reading about live in a version of the real world where you and I go to work or school every day. The superhero operates as a protector and citizen of that world, which skilled creators make us feel is real, no matter how many mutants and aliens appear in a given story. But the key thing is that even if a given superhero is personally psychologically flawed, he or she will rise above their problems to act on their (and our) better qualities. In this way, the superhero represents the best in all of us, the hope that we can be better than our petty needs and desires.

Some other thoughts on superheroes:

- In general, superhero stories tend to resolve their larger conflicts, literally and symbolically, through violence, aka "action," usually in the form of some kind of one-on-one physical conflict. Such a convention might seem to imply that the genre is limited, but I don't believe there are any limits on what a skillful writer and artist can accomplish in terms of superhero stories. Some great superhero tales have been crafted where the conflict is internal or personal, expressed and resolved primarily through dialogue or non-violent action. But superheroes' and supervillains' powers are, indeed, generally most effectively utilized in some kind of visual—physical—conflict, and the shorthand nature of the stories lends itself to such conflict. In whatever manner conflict is expressed and resolved in a given superhero story, however, it will inevitably (and with or without the writer's conscious knowledge) reflect the story's theme (sometimes called the story's "moral" or "message"), which is another way of saying that superhero stories—all stories, really—reveal some universal truth.
- The superhero is a non-religious yet godlike figure who plays out our own problems and challenges in bigger-than-life, operatic terms. The superhero can represent a snapshot of a moment in time in a culture's development, or a broader sense of cultural identity. As a writer, I find superhero stories useful for metaphorically working out, in both literal and symbolic ways, issues that are important to me—and, hopefully, to a lot of other people.
- The superhero story has become a separate, albeit hybrid, genre. It is a mix of science fiction, fantasy, fairy tale, Western, detective, soap opera, romance, and other genres, combined with elements of opera and professional wrestling. The superhero genre, at its best, takes a kids' fantasy and makes it a useful and exciting vehicle for both children and adults to in some way come face-to-face with their own problems and challenges.
- Superheroes are to action/genre heroes as movies are to the arts. They are each hybrids of many things (as noted above). Superheroes require bits and pieces from various genres combined to make something bigger than the parts. Movies require the skills of actors, writers, dancers, musicians, etc. So the superhero genre is a melting pot of other genres. As far as what makes for a superhero as opposed to an action or genre hero: Is John McClane, Bruce Willis' character

in *Die Hard,* an action hero or a superhero? I say he's a superhero, but the line is blurry between super- and action/genre heroes. Ditto for James Bond. Once characters do superhuman things, they're pretty much superheroes. Once they dodge ridiculous quantities of machine gun bullets while their own weapons or abilities never fully give out, they're superheroes, cape or no cape.

- On both commercial and creative levels, codenames are as important as any other part of what makes a given superhero work. The connection between a superhero's codename and his mission or personality has evolved over the generations. Once the basic names—Superman, Spider-Man, Wonder Woman, the Flash—are taken, as they were by the first generation or two of superheroes, then the heroes' codenames become plays on words or expressions of personality traits. Cable, Moon Knight—such names have no real meaning outside the context of their characters' stories. A wolverine was considered perhaps too esoteric an animal after which to name a character in the '40s, but by the '70s being a little esoteric was okay, hence the X-Man of that name. Superheroes' codenames can also serve a function similar to that of various titles and ranks in society. Dr. Smith, Captain Jones, Vice-President Miller, etc.; these identify the individuals' role and place in society. We know (or think we know) what to expect when meeting someone with a title. In many ways, the superheroes' names serve a similar function.

- In the world of commercial superhero creation, the "feel" of a character has as much to do with whether he or she is considered a superhero as any actual powers. Sometimes just co-existing in a story with superhuman beings confers super-status on a character who, in another context, might be considered merely a talented or gifted individual.

Having said all the above, I would also add the hard-to-define quality of "fun" to what makes for an effective superhero. If a character's powers, persona, milieu, and adventures aren't someone's idea of fun, then what's the point? And let's not even get started on what makes a given superhero "cool"...

TWENTY

Superheroes and Power

Dennis O'Neil

Dennis O'Neil, comic book writer and editor, worked at both Marvel and DC. Although he worked on some of the most popular superheroes—Superman, Spider-Man, Wonder Woman, Iron Man, and Daredevil—he is best known for his work on Batman and on Green Lantern/Green Arrow stories, the latter of which raised the bar for social relevance in comic book stories. In addition, he created new Batman villains who continue to plague the Caped Crusader: Ra's al Ghul (co-created with Neal Adams) and Maxie Zeus.

I don't think there's one concise answer to the question, "What is a superhero?" *Hero*, derived from the Greek *heros*, means one who protects and serves. A superhero is that, but it is also a lot more. These days I ask, what evolutionary (i.e., naturally selected) purpose could the notion of "hero" serve? I imagine that the first heroes—probably lost to antiquity—were "descended" from gods. And I think that then—and later—they probably highlighted the values of the society to some degree. The "values of society" element is really obvious with Superman—they put it right at center stage: truth, justice, and the American way. With Captain America, it's the same thing—a kind of national chauvinism.

I think that superheroes have to do with power—identification with power, power that you either have or believe you have, or that you might like to have. In addition, I think they have to do with aspiration. That relates more to Nietzsche's Übermensch: it's not about beating guys up; it's about human perfection. Given the timing of the appearance of Superman and his predecessors, we can assume that superheroes also have something to do with social discontent. In a lot of the crime fiction that appeared following World War I, the protagonists weren't cops. The protagonists were, in one way or another, vigilantes. In some cases, they were actually criminals—Boston Blackie and the Saint, for example. And in lots and lots of cases, they were those guys who bopped around the world and solving crimes, people who were always way smarter than the cops and who didn't have any official standing. This attitude toward police and the establishment in these stories, and in superhero stories as well, symbolically represented that social discontent—the feeling of being powerless and wanting someone to right the world, and of identifying with those figures who had the power to get things done to solve the problems that caused social discontent.

Think about the double-identity motif. It is the readers recognizing their flaws, their limitations, but wanting to identify with something bigger. The imagining or experiencing of the story gives you temporary respite from whatever's bugging you because you can see somebody overcoming a bad situation in the interest of helping somebody like you (or somebody you can pretend to be). The appeal of the superhero has something to do with escape. Lots and lots of people, myself included, were originally drawn to superheroes because something was not right with their lives, or they thought that something was not right with their lives.

There is a kind of priestly aspect to the superhero figure—the costume identifies the wearer with a "higher power." But this function of the costume as a way of marking the wearer works in more ordinary situations as well. Almost every culture has costumes for special occasions. For example, when I put on a tie to get married, it meant it was not an ordinary day; the tie signified that I was the groom and identified me as a participant in the larger cultural institution of marriage—an identification with cultural power. And the priest who married my wife and me put on robes to say he was not himself; he was an avatar of God in that context. The superhero costume functions in a similar way. It signifies a separate identity, one imbued with power, and the superhero figure attracts us because we similarly want to be identified with power; it's a normal part of being human.

I think for a story to count as a *superhero* story, it requires action, it requires the costume motif (although some of the more recent TV shows have gotten away from that), and it requires the ultimate triumph of the protagonist. But mostly it requires that the protagonist do things that an ordinary person cannot do and, by doing them, solve his or her problem.

At some point in superhero stories, either the problem or some aspect of the problem is solved by the heroes' extraordinary abilities. They're doing things that you or I could not do. Moreover, they have the costumes, and they have a reason and a motivation for doing what they do. I think that was often missing in the early superhero stories: The hero beat up the bad guy simply because he was a good guy. The stories at that time were all plot driven because the writers were mostly refugees from the pulps, and the characterizations—such as they were—were tailored to fit the needs of the plot. And it stayed that way for a couple of decades.

When I first went to DC Comics, I think there was really very little in the way of character-driven stories. The first one that I ever wrote was the last *Green Lantern/Green Arrow* story (which appeared in three installments as a back-up story). Oliver Queen really screws up and kills somebody, and the story is what happens as a result of that death—pure character-driven story. I think that currently most of the stories are character driven. The best comic book writers are very much character-driven or character-oriented writers, but they never for a second neglect the needs of the plot. Both things are necessary, and in a well-done story they're inseparable, aligned—the plot is what the character does.

I think of Goethe's criterion for judging any art work: What was the artist trying to do, and did the artist do it? If what you're trying to do is entertain, it's not easy, but it's a different thing than what we were doing with the stories we wrote that called attention to social and cultural problems. But back to what I said earlier about honoring the genre: if you do a superhero story of Batman or Green Lantern and it does not deliver what people normally buy stories about those characters for, you have failed.

A writer fails the genre when a story depicts superheroes who are weak or do not use their powers. What makes a character interesting (both superheroes and other types of characters) is what he does to solve problems. You give him a knotty situation, and he gets out of it. Well, by definition, *superheroes use extraordinary physical means*. And it's fun to watch that stuff. As I said, we always, especially us 71-year-old adolescents, respond to exhibitions of power. *That is what a superhero is.* Batman and Superman would each solve problems in different ways (if the writer were being logical), and they would do it very differently from Ms. Marple or Mike Hammer.* So you have to take that into consideration when creating a story. You cheat your readers if they buy a magazine with a guy in tights and a costume busting through a wall on the cover and you give them some kind of watered-down Henry James story or 22 pages of talk with no action. You have to honor your genre.

Genre can be thought of as a meme, so the superhero genre is a meme. A meme is the cultural equivalent of a gene—it is a unit of ideas, symbols, or practices that can be transmitted from one person to another, just as genes are transmitted from parent to child. I agree with Richard Dawkins's *meme* idea—cultural ideas spread and evolve.

If there's anything that's absolutely true, it's that things change. In the same way that Mike Grell and Frank Miller[†] saw a way to use the superhero meme to express their ideas, I saw a way to use it to write stories about more serious themes. It was stuff I was doing that I was genuinely concerned about. The comic book was the medium that was available to me; all I had to do was figure out a way to use it, and that was not too hard. And it worked out fine. At the same time when I was writing socially relevant stories for *Green Lantern/Green Arrow*, I was also writing stories for *Batman*. With *Green Lantern/Green Arrow*, I was trying to push the envelope with socially relevant stories, but with *Batman* it was pure storytelling. Batman never had an agenda (at least back then) other than to be entertaining. I liked to write both ways.

I think superheroes were in the air at the time of their creation. Superman was much more of a continuation of the heroic idea than a break with the past. Jerry Siegel and Joe Shuster created Superman; you could say that Superman (and therefore the superhero) is a meme, but Lord knows that they did not create it out of whole cloth. Joe and Jerry just drew from a lot of stuff that was in the air. They were big science fiction fans, and costumed heroes already existed or were kind of being co-created with Lee Falk, who created a costumed superhero in the Phantom, and who had no contact with Joe or Jerry. That's the way all this stuff happens: People take a lot of the ingredients that are available to them and figure out a new recipe. A couple of years ago there was a brilliant piece in *Harper's* by Jonathan Lethem making the same point.[‡] You can't be original; what you do is take the old stuff and make it relevant to your audience or figure out a new way to mix the various parts together, and then you apply skill—the skill that you need to communicate that stuff with—and if you're lucky

---

* Editors' note: Both are fictional detectives.
† Editors' note: Both are comic book writer/artists.
‡ Editors' note: "The Ecstasy of Influence: A Plagiarism." *Harper's Magazine*, February 2007. Lethem's piece is an elaborate, witty joke of sorts. All the sentences are taken from other writers' works, albeit with slight revisions. The whole article is, in effect, plagiarized to make Lethem's point that originality and appropriation in art are intimately connected.

you end up with something new. The more I learn about Batman, the less original he seems. Batman's creators Bob Kane and Bill Finger really did a kind of Chinese-menu thing: some choices from one column, some choices from another column. Bill Finger openly admitted that his main inspiration was Walter Gibson's Shadow stories, and the first Batman story in *Detective Comics* #27 was based on Gibson's "Partners of Peril" from a 1936 *Shadow* pulp.*

The popularity of superheroes was originally, I think, based on the novelty of the medium, its strength as a storytelling vehicle, and its iteration of an old kind of fiction that was uniquely visual and which allowed for very compressed storytelling. And everything came together. I think it almost always has to in order for something to become very successful. As Peter Coogan points out in *Superhero: The Secret Origin of a Genre*, the genre was a happy meeting of subject matter and fun. Comic books were, at the time, the ideal medium for this kind of heroic fantasy. Currently, I think that's true of movies. Cinematic technology has caught up with people's imaginations. We used to say in the early days, "What we've got going is that we can do things that movies can't." You want to blow up a planet? Well, in a comic book that'll take a panel, ten minutes, and some ink. Movies couldn't do that in that era. Well, that's obviously not true anymore. Movies *can* do that, and arguably, because motion pictures produce a much more visceral reaction, movies can do it better.

Comics are still evolving, along with everything else, and we're discovering that they have some values we might not have suspected. It'll be interesting to see what's next.

---

* Editors' note: See Robby Reed's three-part series, "Secret Origins of the Batman," in *Dial B for Blog* (http://www.dialbforblog.com/archives/389/) for a rundown of the stories and images Finger and Kane borrowed liberally from to create the first Batman story in *Detective Comics* #27 (cover date May 1939).

TWENTY ONE

The Importance of Context: Robin Hood Is Out and Buffy Is In

Kurt Busiek

Kurt Busiek has written comic book stories for Marvel, DC, Dark Horse, and many other comic book companies. Kurt's most popular works are those that take a fresh look at superhero worlds. In 1993 he wrote the four-issue Marvels series, which looked at Marvel's superheroic universe and its history through the eyes of a regular citizen. Kurt followed this up with his own complex and psychologically rich superhero world and series, *Astro City*.

The question of what constitutes a superhero is, I think, more a philosophical question than a literal one, because when you look for a literal definition—Why is Batman a superhero and James Bond not a superhero? Or is James Bond a superhero? What *is* the definition? Where are the hard-line boundaries?—you get lost in a mire of contradictions. My feeling has always been that "superhero" is one of those vague terms that have certain hallmarks, and a character who has enough of those hallmarks is a superhero. But "enough" is a nebulous term, and not everyone's going to agree on which characters fall where. Still, there are a couple of different ways of looking at the question.

The primary hallmarks of the superhero are *superpowers, costume, code name, secret identity, heroic ongoing mission*, and *superhero milieu*. If the character has three of those six, he or she is probably a superhero. There are characters who don't have powers, like Batman, and there are characters who don't have a code name, like Doc Savage[*] (that's just his name). Dr. Strange[†] is another one. There are characters who don't wear costumes, though some of these, such as the Silver Surfer, have a distinctive visual appearance.[‡] Much more rarely, there are characters who don't have an ongoing heroic mission. If you had just one job to do and you've done it, you're probably not a superhero, unless you have enough of the other elements to overcome that. But a superhero generally makes a career out of his or her mission. The superhero milieu is telling, too—if you take Dr. Strange out of the Marvel Universe, he's a wizard. We have a long literary tradition of stories about wizards, but

---

[*] Editors' note: Doc Savage is Clark Savage, Jr., a pulp adventurer whose adventures were published by Street and Smith from 1933 to 1949 and who has seen numerous paperback and comic book revivals, in addition to being the subject of a campy 1975 feature film, *Doc Savage: The Man of Bronze*, starring Ron Ely. The portrayal of Doc Savage influenced the depiction, and possibly the creation, of Superman.

[†] Editors' note: Dr. Strange is Dr. Stephen Strange, an arrogant neurosurgeon who is injured in a car accident and seeks healing under the tutelage of the Ancient One in the Himalayas, who trains him to be the Master of the Mystic Arts. He is a Marvel Comics character and debuted in 1963.

[‡] Editors' note: The Silver Surfer's body is covered by a silver sheen that allows him to survive in space. Typically he wears no clothing.

we call them fantasies, not superhero stories. If you take the Hulk out of the Marvel Universe, he's a monster. Yet if you put him and Dr. Strange in a superhero milieu where they can join the Defenders, then of course they're superheroes, because they're members of a superhero team. Furthermore, even outside of the Defenders, they're in a world with supervillains, and that world adds a particular kind of structure to the hero-versus-villain story. So we think of Dr. Strange as a superhero, whereas we might not have thought of Mandrake* as a superhero, because Mandrake isn't in that kind of world. Conversely, if we team Mandrake with Flash Gordon† and the Phantom‡ as the Defenders of the Earth, then of course they're superheroes, because once you put that all together you've got a superhero milieu. So the milieu is a contextual aspect of defining the superhero.

To further clarify, I would argue that Flash Gordon isn't a superhero unless you team him up with the Phantom. *Flash Gordon* is a science-fiction adventure series, but Flash Gordon is not a superhero, unless you take the next step in defining the super-hero: A superhero is a hero writ large. By this definition, James Bond is a superhero, and Conan is a superhero, and Flash Gordon is a superhero, because they're just big neo-mythic characters having adventures, and that's how some people apply the term. However, we're covering a different use of the term here. Zorro, though, is a superhero by any measure: he's got a secret identity (dilettante aristocrat), he's got a costume, he's got a code name, and he's got an ongoing mission of justice. He's a superhero because he has the hallmarks of a superhero. He's from 1919, so he predates Superman and Batman. But predating Superman, even predating the use of the term *superhero* as we understand it today, doesn't disqualify Zorro, or other characters, from being superheroes.

The term *superhero* was coined to apply to Superman and Batman and their ilk. There were uses of *superhero* before the creation of Superman, but the meaning we attribute to it today coalesced quickly around Superman, Batman, Captain America, and Wonder Woman—the comic book crowd. Superman is, in a sense, the definitional line for *superhero*. He predates the term in the sense that it came to have meaning as a result of Superman's success and what it spawned. Superman spawned Batman, and Batman spawned Captain America, the Human Torch, and the Sub-Mariner. The pop culture explosion of these characters was distinctive enough to require a special term. They were originally called *mystery men*, but eventually they were called *superheroes*. That's why I call Superman a definitional line—not because there wasn't anybody

---

* Editors' note: Mandrake the Magician is a magician with hypnotic powers who starred in a syndicated comic strip created by Lee Falk starting in 1934.

† Editors' note: Flash Gordon is a science fiction adventurer, created in 1934 in the wake of the success of the Buck Rogers comic strip. In his long-running comic strip, he usually battles Emperor Ming the Merciless to free the planet Mongo. His adventures have also been featured in three serials staring Buster Crabbe, a big-budget 1980 film with Sam Jones, and some low-budget television shows.

‡ Editors' note: The Phantom is a costumed, pulp-style crime-fighter whose comic strip was created by Lee Falk in 1936. The Phantom is often credited as the first costumed crime-fighter in American comics. In 1986, the Phantom, Mandrake, and Flash Gordon were teamed up as the Defenders of the Earth in a syndicated animated television series in which they battled Flash Gordon's foe, Ming the Merciless.

like him beforehand, but because there wasn't a critical mass of characters like that big enough to be recognized as a genre. Once this use of the term became common, it became harder to go back to earlier characters and say that Zorro, the Green Hornet, or the Lone Ranger are not superheroes. In my mind, the Shadow is a superhero, whereas someone like Robin Hood is a borderline case.

Robin Hood has a lot of the characteristics of the superhero. The Robin Hood of legend has an ongoing heroic mission, which is to oppose the injustice of the Sheriff of Nottingham and protect the people of the Sherwood Forest area. He's got a distinctive-looking outfit, though it's not a costume. The Merry Men in some of the legends wear Lincoln green to identify themselves, which constitutes a proto-costume. Robin Hood has a kind of code name, but he doesn't have a secret identity, he doesn't have superpowers, and he doesn't fight supervillains like Dr. Doom. It's easy to push him over the category line, though—if Dr. Doom were to get in his time machine and go back to the time of King Richard to find some buried Arthurian artifact, that would be a superhero story, because Robin Hood would have been placed in a superhero context, a superhero milieu. Working in the reverse direction, if Robin Hood were to fall asleep in medieval times and wake up in modern-day New York, as DC's Arthurian hero the Shining Knight did, then he'd be a superhero. He has enough of the hallmarks to be tipped over the edge by being put in the superhero milieu.

Set in the 12th century, though, it's not so clear. Robin Hood lives in an otherwise realistic world and, aside from being extremely skilled with a bow, isn't superhuman, and there are no other superhumans in his world. With Batman, it's easier to say he's a superhero because there are superhumans around. There's an understanding that in that milieu, characters who do what Batman does are superheroes. Robin Hood's a little squishy; you can argue both sides of the definition with him.

Buffy the Vampire Slayer is a superhero: she has powers, she has a code name— she's "the Slayer," known to the world of monsters by that label—and for a long time she had a secret identity. She also has an ongoing heroic mission. She exists in a world with more than just vampires and demons, as well. It's got cyborgs built by the government, it's got supervillains, it's got all that pulp-explosion adventure stuff that makes up the superhero universe. The only thing she doesn't have is a costume. But she has enough of the standard hallmarks to be a superhero.

So that's one approach to defining the superhero. Genre is another way of looking at what a superhero is, which is one of the reasons that it has vague boundaries. Lots of genres have vague boundaries. What's the difference between horror and fantasy, or science fiction and fantasy? It's hard to say for sure, and there'll be a lot of disagreement about it. It's easy to define the central points, but harder, if not impossible, to define the edge cases. Nevertheless, the superhero is a powerful symbolic character—symbolic of many different things. My big argument, and one of the reasons I created *Astro City*,*

---

* Editors' note: *Astro City* is Busiek's creator-owned comic book, published by Image Comics and DC imprints Wildstorm and Vertigo. *Astro City* stories typically explore how ordinary people react to and live alongside superheroes and supervillains, and they often detail the emotional and psychological states of the superheroes and villains.

is that for years we were told that the superhero represents adolescence—that the superhero is an "adolescent wish fulfillment figure." My reaction to that was, "O.K., if you can do that with a superhero, what else can you do?" Robert Mayer, in his novel *Superfolks*, shows that you can use the superhero as a metaphor for middle age as well.* So the superhero doesn't represent adolescence unless you're using a superhero for that purpose. Superman often represents adolescence, and someone like Spider-Man does so even more literally. Spider-Man's a young adult figuring out how to be responsible in the world and not knowing how to do it yet. And that's adolescence.

The Hulk is more like a four-year-old; there's nothing adolescent about him. He's representative of that age when kids want to be dinosaurs and take great pleasure in imagining great power and destruction, because they're so powerless themselves. He's the world's most powerful baby. For all that, though, you can write stories about Bruce Banner/the Hulk as Dr. Jekyll/Mr. Hyde, with the Hulk representing the unleashed id within—which is a more sophisticated way of coming at the same concept, I suppose. But the Hulk doesn't represent the same things that Superman does, so any question about what the superhero represents has to encompass both these characters and more. I'm firmly convinced that you could write a superhero story in which the superhero represents lost love in the twilight of people's lives, or the positive feelings of the Atomic Age, or the self-identity and pride in emerging African nations in the 1960s (which was done with the Black Panther).† Superheroes are metaphors, and you can pour anything into them. Superheroes are *something* writ large, and that something depends on what you want to write large.

But metaphor alone isn't enough; metaphors abound in other genres. There are stories I've created with the intent that they be superhero stories, only to realize that they could work really well in another context. For instance, I devised a character for a DC series I created called *Power Company*. Her name is Witchfire, and she's a sorceress-homunculus created by a young woman who feels marginalized and unimportant. This woman discovers a magic book that teaches her enough magic to create a construct that can be everything she's ever dreamed of being, so she becomes a famous singer, fashion model, and actress; in addition, she becomes a superhero in order to raise her celebrity Q rating. She's a metaphor for a young person's dreams taking over his or her life, for losing oneself in exterior definitions of success. She doesn't need to be a superhero—if you take her out of the superhero milieu and say she's got magical abilities that she uses to become an actress and a singer and a model, she's rich, and she dates rock stars, you can address the same metaphor and issues. But because she is in a world that has superheroes in it, being a superhero becomes one of the things she can do, and it works fine.

Alternatively, you can create a superhero who has absolutely no metaphorical resonance whatsoever, who's just the spear carrier in the latest issue of *X-Men*—a set of powers, a code name, and a costume, with no more depth than that, and still that's a superhero, albeit probably not a very interesting one. So superheroes can be

---

* Editors' note: *Superfolks* is a novel about a middle-aged superhero with a wife and young children.
† Editors' note: Black Panther, a Marvel character created in 1966, was the prince—and later king—of a fictitious African country, Wakanda.

rich—metaphorical, symbolic, and powerful literarily—and superheroes can be completely empty genre exercises that offer nothing beyond their surface.

So, ultimately, what does it take to make a superhero story? It takes a superhero. You can probably tell a story with a superhero that isn't a superhero story, such as the *Hill Street Blues* storyline involving a lunatic who dresses up like a superhero and calls himself Captain Freedom. The police tolerate him because although he is a crazy lunatic, he isn't actually harmful, and he tries to fight crime. So is he a superhero? He thinks he js. Is *Hill Street Blues* a superhero series? No. In the series, the idea that this guy is actually a superhero is actively rejected. *Hill Street Blues* is about cops doing what they do, and Captain Freedom is an intrusion—both as a concept in the cop genre and as a character within the story—that doesn't work on its own terms. Captain Freedom has a role in that world, but the role is "crazy street lunatic," not "superhero." The storytelling itself rejects the concept of the superhero.

Gotham Central, which is sort of like *Hill Street Blues* in the DC Universe, offers a reverse example. *Gotham Central* is a set of stories about what happens to the supporting characters in a superhero milieu in which Batman fights the Riddler and so forth, so it's just looking at the superhero from a different angle. Those are stories about people who are not superheroes but are living in a superhero setting. Batman's a legitimate superhero in *Gotham Central*, unlike Captain Freedom in *Hill Street Blues*.

So merely having a superhero in a story might be enough, as it is in *Gotham Central*, but it's not necessarily sufficient, as with Captain Freedom in *Hill Street Blues*. In order for a story to be considered a superhero story, the storyteller must accept and make use of the conventions of the superhero genre, such as the prosocial mission, the costume, the code name, and the superpowers. These conventions need to be presented as legitimate options for the characters within the narrative. Otherwise, the superhero is just a moron in a cape, not a functioning genre element. And it's that "functioning genre element" aspect that's important. It would be easy to write a story about a superhero who everybody thinks is a lunatic, like Captain Freedom, and to have the story itself show that this guy's goals are worth something and that his ultimate victory or sacrifice or failure means something. That is, his goals and actions would be validated by the conclusion of the story. If the plot is built around this validation, then the story accepts him as a valid superhero within the narrative, even if the other characters don't.

So if that circles us from the character's symbolic power back to genre elements again, it's probably worth addressing those, at least a little—powers, code name, and so forth. They can function as shallow attributes—that X-Men spear-carrier we discussed earlier—or they can give the character greater resonance, life, and power as a character. I came up with a character called Slick for a series I created called *The Liberty Project*; he serves as a good illustration of the power of the code name. Slick started out as just an idea of a character, completely built on an idea for a power: the ability to remove the friction from things. It was just an emotional idea in the first place, an idea that appealed to me—the thrill of being able to skate or glide down the street, as if ice skating, because there's no friction. So that idea went into a notebook as "the frictionless man," and when I needed to create characters for *Liberty Project*, I pulled it back out and played around with it, and I fastened on the name Slick, because "slick" suggests slipperiness, like an oil slick, which fit the frictionless aspect of it. But then I made him a real fast-talking con-man character, because *slick* also suggests he's a slippery customer, ethically dubious and out for himself. And with that, his powers, his code name, and his personality all meshed together, all worked in the same direction. His superhero attributes add up to a larger picture, rather than simply filling out a checklist of superhero elements. Everything attaches to the same core. That's not strictly necessary, but that's what helps make a superhero memorable and distinctive.

So what's a superhero? As I said at the beginning, I think it's a philosophical question more than a literal one. Approach it from any angle, and you can find exceptions. There is no one single hallmark of the superhero that is universal, and no thematic requirement that you can't find or apply outside the boundaries of the genre. Ultimately, a superhero is a character that we recognize as a superhero, and all the hallmarks are only guidelines. Superman defined the idea, but the countless changes that have been rung on the idea since then (or found in characters that predate Superman) create an environment so broad that it's possible to create a character instantly recognizable as a superhero—imagine a flying, caped company mascot promoting, say, a bank, using all the obvious superhero iconography—and it's also possible to make a case that Robert E. Howard's Conan, who has none of the hallmarks of a superhero, can be called one simply for being a larger-than-life adventure hero who resonates strongly and deeply with an audience.

Where are the boundaries? I'd argue that it doesn't matter. What really matters is not how well a character fits a definition, but how strongly he or she resonates. Characters with strong, resonant ideas at their core will make more of an impact on the cultural consciousness than a character who's just an empty collection of attributes. So it's less about how well characters follow the rules, to my mind, whatever those rules are, and more about how strongly they embody the ideas they're built around.

Employ all the definitional aspects in an unmemorable way, and yeah, the character's a superhero, but who'll care? Make a strong and resonant statement that captures the imagination—like the characters for whom the term was coined—and we'll stretch the definition to accommodate you.

TWENTY TWO

Superheroes Are Made

Tom DeFalco

Tom DeFalco began writing for Archie Comics, moved briefly to DC, and then worked at Marvel for 22 years, where he served as the editor-in-chief from 1987 to 1994. Tom is perhaps best known for his exclusive twelve-year run as creator and then writer of *Spider-Girl* and for his Spider-Man stories. He's also written seminal Thor and Fantastic Four stories. A prolific writer, Tom has created over 200 characters and written hundreds of superhero stories.

What exactly is a superhero? In classical mythology, a hero is anyone who possesses an extraordinary gift. In modern times, it's someone who shows great strength, courage, or some other admirable trait. The term has gotten rather fluid over the years. We currently call baseball pitchers "heroes" for pitching shutouts and call golfers "heroes" for winning tournaments. The same fluidity applies to superheroes. I define a superhero as anyone who possesses a superhuman trait. It doesn't matter whether the trait is a physical one like super-strength or a more cerebral quality like superhuman courage. Captain America might have been a scrawny individual until the super-soldier formula transformed him into an Olympic-level athlete, but it has been established that he trains and exercises many hours each day to keep combat-ready.* If he has any superhuman trait, it's his ability to find a way to succeed—always.

While many people think costumes and secret identities are an essential part of the superhero genre, I do not. They're all accoutrements as far as I'm concerned. I lump them in with secret headquarters, distinctive vehicles, and personalized weaponry. If they fit in with a certain character, fine. If not, forget them. Batman may need a Batmobile, but does Spider-Man really need a Spider-Mobile? Captain America has a shield. The Hulk needs only a pair of pants.

Here's a not-so-secret secret: I love writing superhero stories! There is an incredible freedom to the genre. You can deal with any subject you choose. Ron Frenz and I have produced stories on such topics as prejudice, homosexuality, human trafficking, and physical abuse—all within an "all ages" comic book title. The superhero genre has only two limitations as far as I'm concerned: your own craft and your own imagination. If you're going to write comic books featuring superheroes, you have one additional requirement. Like movies and television, comics are a visual medium. Pictures should be used to tell your story. If it can be told entirely through dialogue, you've written a radio play. The good news is that you don't have to write comic books. You can also write superhero novels, radio plays, or whatever.

---

* Editors' note: Captain America started out as Steve Rogers, a weak man who wasn't fit for war duty; he wanted to do his part, so he volunteered to take a new super-soldier serum. As a result of this serum he became incredibly strong and took on the moniker Captain America.

SUPERHEROES ARE MADE

Some superheroes are born (such as Superman and Thor). Others are the result of hard work, desire, and dedication (such as Batman and Black Widow) or are forced into their roles by events beyond their control (such as Iron Man and Green Lantern). There are also many who become superheroes through a combination of factors (such as Captain America and Daredevil).

But all superheroes share one common trait: they are carefully constructed, structured, and assembled by writers and artists like me and my un-indicted co-conspirator Ron Frenz. We build superheroes like other craftsmen build houses. We begin by selecting a "building site"—a genre that defines the type of story we intend to tell. We lay a firm foundation or theme for the character and his or her series, followed by a framework that explains how our character functions within his or her world. We finish up by adding the necessary accoutrements. Houses require walls, plumbing, and electricity. Superheroes need personalities, powers, subplots, supporting casts, and so on. I will explain the process through the use of four characters: Spider-Man, Spider-Girl, the original Thunderstrike (Eric Masterson), and the new Thunderstrike (Kevin Masterson). Ron and I created three of these characters—the three without major motion picture franchises. Because there are two Thunderstrikes, I differentiate them by calling them Ericstrike and Kevinstrike.

BUILDING SITES

Before beginning any creative project, one must first establish a building site or playground for the story. Is this going to be a story about people who work together in an office or one about a former spy? Do our characters live in the real world or one filled with magic? In fiction, these choices determine the genre of the work, or the category it can most easily be placed within, such as mystery or science fiction. Since our topic is superheroes, let's focus on that genre.

Once you've settled on the superhero genre, you need to choose a sub-genre. Both Spider-Man and Spider-Girl are "friendly neighborhood" web-swingers. The majority of their stories should deal with crimes occurring in or around New York City. You will note that I said "the majority"; both Spider-Man and Spider-Girl have traveled in space, journeyed through time, visited parallel dimensions, and defeated world conquerors.

Ericstrike spent some time physically bonded to Thor.[*] During this period, he dealt with cosmic-level menaces. After he was separated from Thor, his power

---

[*] Editors' note: Thor is a Marvel Comics superhero created in 1962. He is a superhero version of the Norse god, sent to Earth by his father Odin to learn humility. In the late 1980s, Eric Masterson was given Thor's powers and took over the Thor identity; later he took on the independent superhero identity of Thunderstrike. Kevin Masterson is Eric's son and has recently taken on the Thunderstrike identity. (For Marvel fans: an alternate Thunderstrike exists in the MC-2 Universe, but the one discussed here is a new character who is part of the regular Marvel Universe.)

wasn't quite on the same level, so Ron and I focused on "friendly neighborhood" and near-cosmic-level threats. Former Thor sparring partners like the Absorbing Man, Titania, and Juggernaut often proved a little beyond Ericstrike's reach. Ron and I thought of him as the everyman Avenger—the hero who could be you. In contrast, Kevinstrike hovers between near-cosmic-level and cosmic-level threats. (What do you expect from a stubborn teenager who's convinced he already knows everything?)

FOUNDATIONS

Almost everyone knows that Peter Parker was accidentally bitten by a radioactive spider and gained spider powers. But what is the Spider-Man series really about? Is it merely an excuse for the adventures of a colorful superhero, or does it hold a greater meaning? The answer can be found in his origin story in *Amazing Fantasy* #15. After gaining his spider powers, Peter decides to cash in on his new abilities. He designs a colorful costume for himself, uses his scientific expertise to build his amazing web-shooters, and begins a career in show business as the amazing Spider-Man. A burglar later runs past Peter, and Peter doesn't do anything to stop him. This burglar subsequently murders Peter's beloved uncle. After capturing the burglar and turning him over to the police, Peter vows that no innocent will ever again suffer because Spider-Man failed to act. He has learned that "with great power there must also come—great responsibility!" A lot of people get that wrong. They think the line is, "With great power comes great responsibility!" The first version is a universal theme that we have all encountered at some point in our lives. We've been accepted to a new school, joined a new team, been promoted to a new job, or become a parent. We are suddenly thrust into a position of power and must struggle to act in the most responsible manner we can. The second version of the line is nonsense. Just spend a moment or two and think of all the teachers, coaches, bosses, bureaucrats, politicians, or whatever you've encountered over the years who did possess a certain level of power and didn't behave properly. We identify with Spider-Man because he is always struggling to do the right thing. He is constantly forced to choose between serving himself and serving society. The foundation of his series is the struggle to act responsibly, to keep his priorities straight and always act for the greater good, even when it costs him personally.

This struggle is Spider-Man's greatest contribution to the superhero genre. Before he came along, superheroes were generally rich or well-to-do people who already lived exciting lives. Bruce Wayne (Batman) was a multi-millionaire. Hal Jordon (Green Lantern) was a test pilot. Barry Allen (Flash) was a police scientist. They could usually run off to fight crime whenever they wanted. Aside from an occasional problem that usually involved keeping their identities secret from their girlfriends, superheroes before Spider-Man rarely faced any personal difficulties. In contrast, Peter Parker had to attend high school, do his homework, and help support his aged Aunt May. Peter's struggle to act for the greater good despite the personal costs led to some very interesting stories. It eventually became a mainstay for most of the superheroes that followed him and added oceans of depth to the genre.

Spider-Girl handles the responsibility a bit differently, because her foundation is different. In the world of comic books, there are many parallel worlds and alternative universes. One of them depicts a possible future in which Peter Parker marries Mary Jane Watson. They eventually have a daughter who they name after Peter's Aunt May. Forced to hang up his webs after sustaining a crippling injury, Peter continues to fight crime as a member of the NYPD's Crime Scene Unit. Inheriting his spider powers, Peter's daughter eventually follows in his footsteps and becomes Spider-Girl. Having been raised by Peter and Mary Jane, May—or Mayday, as she's called by her friends— takes acting responsibly as a given. She doesn't struggle with the choice between self- lessness and her own desires; she consistently strives to act for the common good. Her series is all about the responsibility of living up to the expectations that she and others have placed on her. She is Spider-Man's daughter and feels the weight of that legacy. Aware only of her father's many achievements, she doesn't realize that he also had doubts, made mistakes, and failed as often as he succeeded. Once again, we're dealing with a universal theme. All of us have goals. Some are realistic; others are not. The struggle to achieve them and the way we deal with our successes or failures define us as individuals. Her struggle is our struggle.

What about Ericstrike? Eric Masterson was an architect. He happened to be pres- ent at a building site when the mighty Thor, the Norse god of thunder, was attacked by a super-menace. During the course of the battle, Eric's left leg was permanently damaged when he instinctively saved a co-worker. Feeling somewhat responsible for Eric's injury, Thor kept an eye on him. The two became friends. A later series of events put Eric at death's door. Thor had only one way to save him: Thor physi- cally and psychically bonded himself to Eric. The architect became the thunder god's human identity. When they eventually separated, Eric was awarded his own enchanted mace and given the name Thunderstrike, although I refer to him here as Ericstrike. Inspired by Thor, Ericstrike wanted to follow the thunder god's lead and help protect his world. He was following a dream—the dream to be a hero like Thor. The Ericstrike series was all about the personal cost of following such a dream or, in fact, any dream. Everyone has dreams. We dream of getting a better job or becoming a writer, musician, actor, or professional athlete. Following your dream can be quite painful at times. It can alienate you from your friends and loved ones, who might not understand your dedication. If you're spending the majority of your time working on your dream, your personal life is going to suffer. During the course of Ericstrike's series, we see him become permanently injured, lose custody of his son, lose his busi- ness, and eventually die. He saves the Earth from destruction and rescues the woman he loves, but he pays the ultimate price for his victories. His story is a metaphor for anyone who struggles to reach a goal. Sacrifices have to be made if you want to become the top student, athlete, salesman, artist, manager, teacher, or whatever. Not everyone is willing to pay the price for success.

At one point, Eric loses custody of his son, Kevin; Kevin then lives with his mother and her new husband. Years after Eric's death, Kevin is presented with Eric's enchanted mace. The teenage Kevin is given the chance to follow in his father's foot- steps. But Kevinstrike isn't Ericstrike. Kevin already knows the high cost of being a superhero and rejects it. Unlike his dad, Kevin doesn't believe in superheroes. He resents them for allowing his father to die. He also has mixed feelings about his dad. Intellectually, Kevin knows Eric did the right thing by sacrificing himself to save the planet. Emotionally, he's still dealing with abandonment issues, still angry that his father chose being a superhero over raising a son. The Kevinstrike series is all about the struggle to accept the past so that you can move forward into a better future. Everyone has been wronged or disappointed or suffered a personal tragedy. We can wallow in the past and let it hinder or consume us, or we can find a way to accept what's already happened, learn from it, and choose to move forward. Kevinstrike isn't bound by Ericstrike's mistakes or doomed to suffer the same fate. Like all of us, he can choose his own path and become his own person. His journey is the foundation of his series.

FRAMEWORKS

When Spider-Man was first introduced to the world, he was in high school. We watched as he grew old enough for college. He eventually graduated and began looking for a job. He is still trying to figure out what he wants to be when he grows up. The initial framework was built on the idea that it was perfectly natural for a student to struggle with responsibility. Some people think he never should have aged past high school or college. I respectfully disagree. The struggle to accept one's responsibilities is never over. The secret to this framework is to keep piling obligations on Peter's back and, just when he looks like he's about to topple from the weight, add a few dozen more!

Peter also feels responsible for his uncle's death. If only he had stopped that fleeing burglar, Uncle Ben would still be alive. Peter learned that when he fails, people die. This is an important part of Spider-Man's framework because it colors every decision he makes. Because he is afraid of failure, Peter tends to second-guess himself. He can see a dark cloud behind every silver lining. This tendency has given a lot of people the mistaken impression that Peter is a loser. He isn't. He just sees himself that way. Peter's negativity makes him one of the most courageous superheroes of all. He enters every battle believing that he can lose it, but he goes anyway.

Like her father, Spider-Girl is also in high school when her story begins. In contrast to her dad's development, Ron Frenz and I have decided to keep her there. We believe the kinds of people and the problems one faces in high school are repeated in one form or another throughout one's life. Spider-Girl first dons her costume when an old enemy rises to get revenge on her dad. She saves her father and learns a lesson that is different from Spider-Man's: when she succeeds, people live. It's a subtle but profound difference that allows Spider-Girl to approach being a superhero in a much more optimistic frame of mind. As the daughter of Mary Jane, Mayday has a lot more confidence than Peter. She believes in herself and trusts her instincts. She isn't afraid of failure and rarely second-guesses herself. No matter what she's facing, she'll find a way to beat it. That's what spider-people do!

The framework for the Ericstrike series was architect/builder by day and warrior/destroyer when needed—with all the action and angst we could muster!

Because Kevinstrike is all about the struggle to shake off the shackles of the past and find a new future, Ron Frenz and I decided to set his series in high school. We've also given him a special teacher. Gruenhilda, or Grunny (named to honor the legendary Marvel editor Mark Gruenwald), is a Valkyrie sent from the home of the Norse gods to teach Kevinstrike how to use his enchanted mace properly. Because she's as new to Earth as he is to being a superhero, they have a lot to teach each other. Steve Rogers, the original Captain America, also appears in Kevinstrike's series as a kind of Merlin to Kevin's King Arthur.

ACCOUTREMENTS

When we first meet Peter Parker, we learn that he is a hard-working honor student who lives with his Aunt May and Uncle Ben. Although he's described as shy, we learn that he has repeatedly attempted to date the beautiful Sally Avril. She refuses him, preferring athletes like Flash Thompson. Each of these details adds another layer to the character of Peter Parker. He might be introverted, but he isn't timid. He might not be a member of the popular crowd, but that doesn't stop him from approaching the prettiest girls. As Spider-Man, Peter is given some pretty standard powers. He gains enhanced speed, agility, and strength. He also gets the ability to stick to walls. His sole unique power is his uncanny spider-sense—a tingling in the back of his head that warns him of danger and makes it virtually impossible for anyone to sneak up on him. In many ways, Spider-Man is defined by his spider-sense. Because he moves nearly 40 times faster than the average man and his spider-sense warns him of approaching fists, hitting him isn't easy. Spider-Man is a hero who relies on his instincts. Thinking can only slow him down. I've always believed that's why he cracks so many jokes. He's trying to distract his enemies and himself.

Peter eventually discovered that he could make money by taking pictures of himself as Spider-Man and selling them to the local newspaper, the *Daily Bugle*, which resulted in an army of supporting characters based at the paper, including publisher J. Jonah Jameson. This accoutrement opened up numerous avenues for stories and also gave Peter a regular excuse to don his costume and go out as Spider-Man.

Spider-Girl doesn't need any such excuse. She already accepts the fact that she has a responsibility to protect her "neighborhood" as Spider-Girl. When we first meet May, we are introduced to her supporting characters: a few high school athletes (Brad Miller, Moose Mansfield, and Davida Kirby) and a couple of honor students (Courtney Duran and Jimmy Yama). Unlike her dad, she straddles the boundary between these high school worlds easily, and each mirrors a different side of Mayday's personality. The purpose of such supporting characters is to give us insight into our main character— both her civilian and her costumed personas—and to provide story fodder. Being a teenage girl, Spider-Girl doesn't behave like a boy. Spider-Girl takes a non-violent route whenever possible, preferring to talk to her enemies instead of fighting with them. Her tact often works, resulting in her becoming friends with former foes.

Ericstrike, had a life and his own cast of characters before he met Thor—a son, an ex-wife, her new husband, a personal assistant, a lawyer, and even a few good friends. Eric was a decent man whose life revolved around his son and his work, at least until Thor entered his life. Like Spider-Girl, he didn't need an excuse to go out as a superhero. He went out when he was bonded to Thor because that was the thunder god's will and nobody argues with an Asgardian wielding an invincible magic hammer. After being separated from Thor, he went out because that's what Thor trained him to do.

When we first meet Kevin Masterson, we learn that he's a school bully. He's a troublemaker who has already been thrown out of a few schools. In the Kevinstrike series, Ron and I are in some ways asking what would have happened if Flash Thompson (the high school bully in Spider-Man) had been bitten by that radioactive spider.* What if an angry young man with unresolved father issues gained the power of a thunder god? Would he use his new abilities to make peace with the past, or would he lash out? Those are some of the questions Ron and I will delve into in Kevin's new Thunderstrike series.

As you can see, the accoutrements for superheroes are all the little details and layers of personality that make them believable, give them a sense of reality, and make the readers care about them. A character's costume might be cool, his weapons impressive, and his powers unique, but his or her personality is what will draw readers back to him or her month after month. Spider-Man and Spider-Girl have costumes, powers, and weaponry that reflect a spider motif. Thunder and lighting are evoked by Ericstrike and Kevinstrike. Costumes, powers, and weaponry are all necessary, but they are not the most important factors that go into creating superheroes. They are just additional details. They must suit the character because fiction, any fiction, revolves around its characters.

MAKING THE HOUSE A HOME

We have discussed some of the elements that go into creating superheroes, but what's the point? Do superheroes really matter? I think they do. Although they currently appear in movies, on television, in video games, and in a host of new media, the superhero's primary home is in comic books. I believe comic books may very well be the last true bastion of short fiction in this country. As the dominant genre in this distinctly American art form, superheroes are important.

Like every other kind of fiction, stories about superheroes tell us something about the human condition. They help us make sense of the world around us. Real life can seem pretty random at times. Pipes can burst, cars can suddenly crash through your living room wall, and the people you love can die without warning. Anything within the laws of science can happen. In fiction, there are no random events; every element of a story has a purpose.

Superheroes also present us with idealized versions of ourselves. They possess the physical and mental attributes, the courage, and the honor we wish we had. They

---

* Editors' note: This possibility was explored in *What If?* #7 (cover date February 1978) in a story titled, "What If Someone Else Had Become—the Amazing Spider-Man?"

routinely stand up to evil and injustice. They face unstoppable super-menaces but still find a way to overcome them in 22 pages. They show us that no problem, no matter how great, no matter how overwhelming, is truly insurmountable. That's why we love our superheroes. They never accept defeat. If they can always find a way to succeed, so can we. Although we might never possess super-strength, courage, honor and any other admirable trait is always within our grasp. We just have to believe in ourselves.

TWENTY THREE

Extraordinary

Joe Quesada

Joe Quesada had already established his impressive career as a comic artist, drawing for Marvel, DC, Valiant, and his own Event Comics, before becoming editor of *Marvel Knights* and then taking the helm of Marvel Comics as editor-in-chief and then chief creative officer of Marvel Entertainment. While editor-in-chief, Quesada brought in artists and writers who did not traditionally work on superheroes, thus shifting the Marvel aesthetic.

What is a superhero? It's a question that has a wide range of responses depending on the era and society in which a particular superhero was conceived. Historically, we could go back to the myths and stories of Hercules or Beowulf, or perhaps even further to the ancient hunter, sitting by the fire, regaling his tribe with tales of the great expedition. Even the caveman, painting on dimly lit walls, did his best to tell us stories of the great god of the hunt. More recently, of course, we can find the vestiges of this type of story within the idea and creations of the American superhero and thus, in a very American "melting pot" sort of way, add to its modern definition. This tangled history makes trying to distill the superhero down to a singular definition a bit difficult, but to me, looking at it through the lens that is Marvel, a superhero is simply *an extraordinary person placed under extraordinary circumstances who manages to do extraordinary things to ultimately triumph over evil.*

The traditional superhero as we know it today—the super-powered, costumed, comic book variety—is something that is unique to and originated in America. By that I mean that it takes the idea of a classic character like Hercules and applies—or tries to apply—a rational reason and origin for why the superheroes are so extraordinary—whether it be genetics, chemistry, or place of origin (as in the case of Superman, who is an alien from another planet). Many classic hero tales and myths didn't have the type of origin story that was grounded in the real world. I think that's something unique about superheroes and the way that they were constructed here in America—that and the fact that they wear their underwear on the outside, but even that particular look is something that is rooted in real people. The now-standard superhero costume expanded on the outfits of circus performers, athletes, and gymnasts as they were seen back in the day, Superman and Batman being perfect examples. And the costume is definitely part of the appeal of the superhero—the bright primary colors, the whole silhouette of the character standing there in a heroic pose, cape flapping in the wind. It's colorful, theatrical, and, yes, reminiscent of the strong men or circus performers who were popular when the first American superheroes were introduced.

If I put myself in the context of those times, it becomes very clear to me that the American superhero was truly revolutionary. Superman, for example, was a real discontinuity relative to the existing heroes of the time. He signaled a different type of hero—a hero who was more than human—in contrast to characters such as the Phantom or Zorro. Zorro was just a great athlete, a swordsman. He had a very heroic outlook on life and wanted to serve the downtrodden, but he had no superpowers. What he did have, however, was a secret identity. But Superman took the secret identity, the costume, the cape—a look that was somewhat commonplace amongst pulp heroes—and added superpowers and a compelling origin and back-story. That combination was wholly new at the time, and it is the reason that the character resonated so strongly with readers of the day.

Around that time, the term *superhero* was much easier to define. Colorful costume, extraordinary powers, and a secret identity—the formula was basic and, with perhaps a few exceptions, almost universal. Today, the lines are blurred considerably. One could argue that in the film *Die Hard*, Bruce Willis's character is a superhero. He's basically doing superheroic things. Although he doesn't claim to have, nor is it hinted at that he has, superpowers, he does manage to do things that no ordinary human could ever attempt while reasonably thinking he or she could survive. So today, I think that modern superhero stories are defined more by the amazing circumstances and the trials and tribulations that the heroes have to face, circumstances that are beyond the norm and with outcomes that affect a wide magnitude of people—sometimes the world in general.

In addition to this new interpretation, I find that even a secret identity isn't as necessary as it was in decades past. It used to be that every superhero kept his true identity secret, like Zorro, Batman, and Spider-Man. It was a formula that was almost habitual when creating a hero. That contrivance has subsided in some ways, or at least it is no longer considered a given or a must; today we have superheroes who are out in the open, as made evident by very popular franchises like the X-Men and the Fantastic Four. Even Tony Stark (Iron Man) went public, because the secret identity didn't make sense for him. There was a time when revealing a hero's secret identity was considered a story element to avoid, but today it's open to debate if it serves the character in better ways.

Different types of superheroes fill different roles for different eras and audiences. Going as far back as the time of the creation of Superman and Batman, superheroes were all perfect and paternal. In the 1960s, Stan Lee took that paradigm and turned it around. He wanted to create superheroes with problems—superheroes who weren't necessarily the most handsome or idealized person in the story. In essence, he developed superheroes who were more relatable. This marked, without question, the greatest shift in the concept of not only the American superhero, but the American hero in general. It's a shift that, in the era and decades that followed, marched in lockstep with the American disillusionment with its "real world" heroes.

Today, the sky is the limit when creating a superhero and trying to define what role he or she might fill. We even have superheroes who are hugely dislikable people; some of them come from really bad circumstances, and some started as villains. They might not necessarily seem like the hero of story, but in the end they always teach us a moral lesson. During my tenure at Marvel, a lot changed, and some ideas were reinforced by the events of 9/11. It was right at that time that we saw that the difference between a character like Spider-Man and someone who was actually there at Ground Zero—a firefighter, a policeman, a rescue worker—is wafer thin. That day changed everybody's perspective on what heroes are and what superheroes should be, as well as the way we tell their stories.

I think superheroes also represent different aspects of our lives; in many ways they're metaphors for us or an idealization of what we want or hope to be. We all seek a bit of wish fulfillment, and that's a very big aspect of the superhero ideal. In the Marvel sense of it, superheroes are built very much to be the reader in that they are normal people. We focus on the alter ego—the "human" character—before the super side. It is the normal person who is able to put on a costume and become more than what he or she is that is the most important part in the Marvel equation.

That's why for me in these modern times, the alter ego is all-important. The creation of a superhero comes together best when we have a really solid foundation with respect to the alter ego. I had a conversation with Stan Lee during one of my first weeks as Marvel Editor-in-Chief. We were talking about stories and Marvel heroes, and I decided to ask Stan (not really believing he'd have an answer in his back pocket), "If you could distill the formula for creating a perfect Marvel hero, what would that formula be?" Stan said, "Imagine it's a dark stormy night, and there on a precipice of a building is Spider-Man. He's about to leap into the urban canyon below. Really at the end of the day, it's just a red and blue suit standing at the precipice of that building. But if you tell us about that guy in the suit, if you tell us who Peter Parker is—who he loves, who loves him, what his problems are, is he going to school, is he trying to hold down a job, who are his friends—if you tell us all these things about him, then when he leaps off that building, our hearts race because we're in that costume with him; we're there with him and can relate to him. He's not just an empty suit." That's really something that we still do to this day. We have to make the alter ego someone we care about.

To do that, we start with the alter ego. We might have an idea for a particular superhero character, but if we can't make the alter ego of that character compelling, then when all is said and done, we've failed. To me, every issue of *Spider-Man* is really an issue of *Peter Parker*. Every issue of *Iron Man* is really an issue of *Tony Stark*. That's where we start. When you throw in the fantastic—the costume element, the super-power element—it now isn't the thing you hang your story on but rather the frosting on the cake that helps to enhance the story. So for me, in the creation of a modern superhero, I personally start there. I want to know who these people are. Then, based upon who they are, where they live, eventually—through the process of creation—they develop their own personality, they develop ethnicity, they develop characteristics that make them more human.

A great example is a character we created called Araña (a spinoff character from Spider-Man). She's a young girl in high school who, through a series of machinations, finds herself with powers similar to Spider-Man's. Somewhere in the process of creation, we came to the idea that this character grew up and lived in the Greenpoint section of Brooklyn, and her father was the superintendent of a building. As things started to come together and aspects of her personality started to become clearer, the character started to remind us more and more of the woman who was my assistant at the time. My assistant was of Puerto Rican and Mexican descent, and before you knew it, we suddenly had an ethnicity for the character. This also started to give us more ideas about her personality and origin. From there we eventually got her name: now that she was of Latin descent and spoke Spanish fluently, the logical thinking would be that she would take on the name Araña (Spanish for *spider*), as that would speak volumes to her personality and passion for her culture. Once those pieces were in place, her look came just as organically and also reflected her personality, age, ethnicity, and geographic location.

This way of constructing the superhero makes him or her more relatable. As a kid, I always found the construction of Marvel characters to be more honest because, if you looked at Superman or Batman, you saw two characters whose "normal" alter egos, Clark Kent and Bruce Wayne, were actually facades—Superman and Batman are the "real" persons. In other words, they have metaphorically lied to us in order to walk among us and become relatable to the people in their world. Superman has to dumb himself down—he has to become clumsy Clark Kent; he bumbles around and is anything but super. It's the same thing with Batman. Bruce Wayne died the day his parents were murdered, and the "real" person, Batman, merely uses the Bruce Wayne persona in order to facilitate his deeds. Stan Lee took that idea and turned it on its ear to get what I believe is a more accurate and honest one: Peter Parker is Peter Parker, and, like so many of us, he'll put on a mask to become someone else, something other than who he really is. At the office I put on my "Editor-in-Chief" mask. When I go home, I put on my "Daddy" mask for my daughter. We all have different faces that we put on for different roles in life; that's what Peter Parker and so many Marvel heroes do. It's another aspect of the modern superhero that has now become an established pillar of their construction because, inherently, it's the stronger idea.

The alter ego is important for the villain as well as the superhero. When a story is working properly in my world, the construct of the alter ego of the villain and that of the superhero are very similar; they're almost the same person, except that at one point in their lives one person took the road to the left, and the other one took the road on the right. One need look no further than a character like Doctor Doom, who is essentially a version of Reed Richards* who lived a slightly different life, took a different road, and now has a different perspective on life. When that happens with a villain and a hero, you end up with iconic rivals—those characters that fans will always see as part and parcel of one another, because they are basically different sides of the same coin.

Let me say a bit about superhero movies. Because these movies are now so prevalent and reach a wider audience, the idea of the American superhero is currently going global. Up until the recent success of superhero movies in Hollywood, the concept of the superhero had lived in a cultural ghetto for a very, very long time. Those of us who lived in this ghetto knew that the source material was no different from, and just as

---

* Editors' note: Reed Richards (also known as Mr. Fantastic) is one of the Fantastic Four; he and Doctor Doom are both highly intelligent inventors and met in college.

powerful and significant as, Beowulf, classic Greek mythology, or any of the heroic tales of antiquity. But there seemed to be a certain embarrassment on the part of the American mainstream about the idea of superheroes. There was a prejudice against the material, a belief that it was a lesser art form. During this time, if you weren't a fan of superheroes and someone asked you, "Hey, what do you think of comics?" you'd probably say, "That's a child's medium; they're for little kids." Those of us who are fans of the medium know that for the past 20 years that hasn't been the case at all. Comics have been a highly sophisticated art form with incredibly mature material. Meanwhile, I would look in frustration at movies like *Die Hard* and think, "Well, that's a superhero movie, he's just not wearing a costume." Hollywood was already telling superhero stories; they were just doing it without some of the more fantastical elements. Now, we're in a world where Hollywood is run by so many who have been weaned on these stories, the spiritual creative sons and daughters of Stan Lee who have grown up loving these stories and wondering why they have never been considered material for or done well on the big screen. And here we are, out of the ghetto and in a theater near you with an almost fanatical reverence for the source material. Hollywood has caught up and brought the mainstream with it. And I can assure you, if Officer John McClane* ever graces the silver screen again, some Hollywood exec is going to think out loud, "Hey, maybe we should put a cape and costume on him; it'll double the box office."

---

* Editors' note: John McClane is the name of Bruce Willis's character in the *Die Hard* films.

TWENTY FOUR

The Superprotagonist

Fred Van Lente

Fred Van Lente has become known for taking his own irreverent tack on classic superhero characters, including four sets of Marvel Zombies, the swinging C-list supervillain heist book *MODOK's 11*, the humorous *Incredible Hercules,* and the conspiracy satire *Archer & Armstrong* for Valiant Comics. In addition, his retelling of the history of the comic book industry in *The Comic Book History of Comics* and of the lives of great thinkers in *Action Philosophers* shows that he has a deep (albeit deeply humorous) side as well.

This essay is the edited transcript of a phone conversation between Van Lente and the editors that took place on October 1, 2010.

What is a superhero? I am vastly more interested in addressing the *super* part than the *hero* part, so I would have to say that a superhero is any protagonist (of any story) with more than mortal abilities. I know that casts too broad a net for some, but that's how I would define it.

Just as there's no such thing as a protagonist in real life, to me there's no such thing as a hero. My problem with "hero" as it's used in the superhero world is that it's a job description, which seems terribly simplistic to me. I haven't met a soldier or a police officer who takes that kind of high praise of his profession without a grain of salt, much less describes herself that way. Most of them know that like any job, there are good soldiers and bad soldiers and good cops and bad cops, although obviously the good are vastly in the majority. When a person begins to think of himself or herself as a hero all the time, it inevitably leads to hubris, corruption, and all sorts of unpleasant things.

I guess that's why I enjoy writing about villains so much. To me it's more dramatically interesting to move a character out of his comfort zone. A rogue acting heroic is going to surprise herself as much as the audience; a guy who just wakes up every morning and puts on his mask and cape and looks for bank robberies to foil is just doing what he does naturally. Morbius the Living Vampire, one of the stars of my *Marvel Zombies* books, is the classic example of a character who started out as a Spider-Man villain and then became a hero in his own right. The supervillains of *Taskmaster* and *MODOK's 11* are good examples, too. Partially I'm just attracted to crooks as a personality type, because I've kind of been a compulsive troublemaker my whole life, but mostly because they problematize a largely phony Manichean notion of good and bad.

I converted an entire hero team into villains in *X-Men Noir*, a book I did with artist Dennis Calero. The series basically asks the question, what if the X-Men franchise had been created in the 1930s as a pulp crime series instead of in the 1960s as a teen superhero series?* One of the first decisions we made was that there weren't going to be any powers

---

* Editors' note: Marvel's noir series reimagined leading Marvel characters in a 1930s setting, in a film noir or parboiled style reminiscent of pulp fiction from the 1930s. In addition to the *X-Men Noir* series, Daredevil, Wolverine, Luke Cage, Iron Man, and Spider-Man were all given the noir treatment.

in the book,* which was fairly radical, but I thought it would be interesting to take all the superpowers out of a superhero story and see what happens. I brought in eugenics, which was such a big topic of concern in the early 20th century, the notion that criminal traits were racial and/or inherited, and used that in place of the idea of the "mutant" from the original X-Men. In our book, the *Noir* version of Professor X runs the Xavier School for Exceptionally Wayward Youth in Westchester, New York, in a purposefully vague neo-Depression era. Instead of reforming juvenile youth, he develops their sociopathic tendencies, because he believes the aggressiveness and cunning of the sociopath is the next state in human behavioral evolution.

Conversely, Dr. Xavier diagnoses the Angel, the hero of the series, who has had a seriously damaged childhood, with *heropathy*, a compulsion to right wrongs and embody in himself a sort of permanent heroic model.† But it turns out that Angel is in fact two brothers playing the same costumed role, and one brother is much more disturbed than the other. One brother—the "bad" one—is killed, and in the sequel, *X-Men Noir: Mark of Cain*, his personality seems to overwhelm over the "good" brother and make him start to act in brutal, almost villainous ways. It's as if the heroic brother can't exist without the villainous one, so he internalizes the villain as part of his own personality.

Dr. Xavier's diagnosis of Angel seems accurate to me because in my opinion, only a disturbed person would put on a cape and run around at night beating up criminals. A normal person would avoid this kind of lifestyle, if only because, you know, it takes up a lot of time and kind of prevents you from developing normal relationships.

I'd say Peter Parker is an example of someone who's disturbed in this way. When I was writing *Amazing Spider-Man*, I loved putting Peter in situations where he had to help out his friends, because Peter is unusually guilt motivated. The weight of the world presses down on Peter's shoulders after the death of his Uncle Ben.‡ This tragedy leaves Peter an emotionally disturbed individual who cannot move on with his life. I was able to have Peter Parker's ex-girlfriend Mary Jane Watson say things like, "You know, you didn't shoot Uncle Ben, it was that other guy. You should stop acting like you did and live your life like a normal person." And that's a point I really wanted to drive home. These hero people have issues!

So, like I said, I'm vastly more interested in "super" than "hero," partly because the exciting part of that "super," for a writer, is there really aren't any limits to what can fit into the genre. This is particularly true in the Marvel Universe, where you have

---

* Editors' note: In the regular X-Men series, each of the X-Men has some mutant-based super-power. In that series, Professor Charles Xavier, the leader of the X-Men, runs a school for exceptionally gifted youngsters in which students learn to master their mutant powers.

† Editors' note: The Angel from *X-Men Noir* is not the winged mutant from the regular X-Men series, but a superhero who debuted in *Marvel Comics* #1 (October 1939). He is a non-superpowered detective who wears a blue costume with a red cape, similar to Superman's.

‡ Editors' note: Peter Parker feels guilty about his uncle Ben's death because Peter's lapse in good judgment inadvertently led to a series of events that culminated in a thief murdering Ben (first told in *Amazing Fantasy* #15).

mythology mixing with science fiction, mixing with pulp avenger figures; you can have Hercules running around doing pseudo-superhero stuff in modern day, while he's flashing back to the well-established myths of his labors and other adventures that he's been through in his past. (That was one of our main shticks in *Incredible Hercules*.) At Marvel, you can throw in any element from anything that's ever been written, ever—and people have—and that's the beauty of the superhero genre; it's this wonderful melting pot of stuff from across all cultures, from all forms of fiction. That's what makes it such a wonderfully American genre—it's this beautiful muddle.

Any good genre is ductile enough to encompass just about any subject matter or theme. If there are limitations to the superhero genre, it is because to a certain extent the core readership historically has been disenfranchised males. So the superhero genre tends to fall into revenge fantasies, and there's a lot of posturing. That, to me, is the negative side of the genre; it turns into what O'Brien, the inner-party character in George Orwell's *1984*, says when he describes Big Brother's culture:

> Always there will be the intoxication of power, constantly increasing and constantly growing subtler. Always, at every moment, there will be the thrill of victory, the sensation of trampling on an enemy who is helpless. If you want a picture of the future, imagine a boot stamping on a human face—forever.[1]

So it comes down to who is wearing the boot and who is getting kicked in the face. To me that's a horribly reductive way of looking at life and human relationships. The biggest sin of the superhero genre is that it can turn into —at its worst, and even sometimes at its best—"Whose ass are we kicking and why do they deserve to have their asses kicked?" So the genre can be very reductive and very primitive.

You can trace the evolution (or devolution) of the power fantasy from the genre's very beginnings. Superman was great because his creators, Jerry Siegel and Joe Shuster, cleverly started with science fiction concepts but grounded them in the trappings of the pulp fiction heroes to make the Krypton space stuff something everyone could relate to—particularly kids, who are constantly constrained by powerful forces above them. Superman is someone who can just shrug off any outside restriction, which is very powerful wish fulfillment. What Siegel and Shuster discovered with Superman was a new way to fulfill an age-old desire.

I'm going to take an unpopular stand and admit that I've never liked Superman. It probably has something to do with the costume. I don't like costumes. I've never liked costumes. That's always been the hardest aspect of superheroes for me. There is a scene in the third issue in *Incredible Hercules* where Hercules is caught in a jet fuel explosion that burns off all of his clothes. I suggested, "Let's burn all his clothes off, burn all his hair off. Let's give him a track suit and keep him bald, and have him run around in a track suit for the rest of the series." Everyone went berserk, including Greg Pak, my co-writer, so they put the kibosh on that one. Oh, well. I constantly want to get characters out of their stupid costumes.

We started out talking about converting heroes into villains; in a book called *Taskmaster* we went in the opposite direction and converted a bad guy into a good guy—or, I guess more accurately, showed how a bad guy could be a good guy all along without realizing it himself. Taskmaster is an *Avengers* villain George Perez and David Michelinie created back in 1980. His superpower is "photographic reflexes": if he watches Spider-Man fight, he can remember those moves and then fight like Spider-Man. And he's gone through the same process watching Daredevil, Captain America, Iron Fist, and all sorts of superheroes on CNN or whatnot. I was asked to put him in his own book, which means that he is the protagonist and therefore no longer a supervillain by my definition. He is the superhero. Taskmaster has trained villains and worked through various bad-guy organizations, but a rumor starts that he has turned state's evidence and is now a double-agent working for the heroes. The Org—the villain underground—puts a billion-dollar bounty on his head, so Taskmaster is fighting his former students, who start attacking him to cash in on the bounty. He goes on a quest across the Western hemisphere to find the Org and force them to cancel the bounty. Here's the catch: we learn that a side effect of Taskmaster's powers is that his photographic memory ends up erasing what neurologists call episodic memory—the memory of things that have actually happened to him, his own past.

The story focuses on his learning his secret origin, the origin so secret that not even he knows it. I needed some explanation for why he's in costume because I hate costumes, which is because of his memory loss, because people are constantly walking up to him and saying hello and he has no idea who they are. He wears a mask all the time so he can pretend to know more than he does and disguise his expression so people won't realize when he's surprised. The costume is essentially an expression of weakness. In writing his story, I researched a lot about Alzheimer's patients; one of the things that they do is start lying to make it seem as if they remember more than they actually do. Over the course of the story, you learn that Taskmaster started as a hero—as an agent for S.H.I.E.L.D. I won't give away the whole book, but you find out that he underwent an experimental treatment to improve his memory, which resulted in his superpower of photographic reflexes but had the side effect of his losing his memories of his wife and the life that he had before. He forgot that he was a good guy. That guilt stays with him every time he loses his memory, which happens every time he has to learn a new skill. He immediately reverts to being a villain because of all of the pent-up feelings of guilt, that he's done something wrong, what neurologists call "illusion of truth." This leads him to conclude that he's a bad guy, when in fact he's always been a good guy.

It's a fun project, one of my favorites I've written for Marvel. It's what I enjoy most: putting superhero tropes into the taffy machine, stretching them out and twisting them around, and seeing what sort of cool new shapes we can form.

NOTE

1. George Orwell. (2004). *1984*. Fairfield, IA: 1st World Library, p. 334.

TWENTY FIVE

Superheroes and Supervillains: An Interdependent Relationship

Ivory Madison

Ivory Madison is the author of, among other works, *Huntress: Year One*, from DC Comics, a "feminist-mafia-noir-superhero graphic novel" origin story. She is the CEO and Editor-in-Chief of Red Room, a social media platform and online community for successful authors. Before that, Madison founded The Red Room Writers Society, where she taught writing and personally coached hundreds of writers on the nature of heroes and villains. We asked her to address the role of the supervillain in defining the superhero.

In literature and in life, the villain defines the hero by taking actions that require the hero to make moral choices in response. The hero observes bad acts by the villain and judges the villain. The hero decides not only to be unlike the villain, but also to stop him or her. And so "our hero" starts out as a potential hero, theoretically and inarticulately "good." The story really begins when she must prove it in a consequential way that involves risk. Even if the hero has already proven to be heroic in the past, it doesn't matter. She must now rise to a higher level of heroism as a result of the villain's choices. Most heroic characters are self-directed (they identify and face evil alone) and have noble aspirations (they have a sincere mission to protect others). In real life, being both totally self-directed and selflessly noble is unusual. Those who can do it really do get labeled as heroes. Our concept of this paradoxical ideal personality is the fixation of storytelling. We want to be heroes.

Heroes tend to follow the Golden Rule, but villains don't. The problem one faces as a writer is that because of the non-negotiable tenet that the hero is good, the hero is at a natural disadvantage. The writer must overcome this disadvantage without resorting to *deus ex machina*. All of the characters spring from the head of their creator, and so resolving these dilemmas, legitimately or not, reveals a great deal about the writer.

If we read a story or see a film in which the hero is entirely alienated from and simply shoots all his opponents, we know it's not great storytelling. He may be the winner, but that's a different matter than being a hero. Another easy way out for writers is to make the bad guys so bad that the hero has no moral dilemma in killing or hurting them. Yet rather than having the hero face a sadistic Nazi SS officer, wouldn't it be more interesting if he were facing a working-class soldier in the German army who is protecting his wife's Jewish relatives from being killed? I've also noticed that villains often fail in literature because their creators believe they have to. But there has to be a meaningful and authentic reason that a believable hero wins against a believable villain, or else the story feels formulaic.

In most of my stories, a reluctant hero knows that she has to do more to live a meaningful life, that she needs to pursue something she knows is her life's biggest challenge, something that will protect others, and that it will put her at great risk. In my stories, the villains are usually symptoms of a political or social system so vast and impenetrable it seems impossible to bring it down. Somehow, and usually reluctantly, the hero finds it within herself to confront the forces of evil, although it's rarely clear whether she will win.

The tradition has been to depict strong female characters—from mythology to epic poetry to movies to comics—as villains or harpies or anything but heroic. The visionary exception was Wonder Woman, created explicitly to counteract traditional views of women. These depictions made it difficult for the average female audience member to identify with strong female characters and left women to choose between identifying with men who either used or rescued women and identifying with women who were bad or irrelevant. Catwoman was originally written as a villain, but her appeal to readers, and to Batman, evolved as our culture evolved, and she is now a strong and respectable hero. Members of other marginalized groups have had a similar challenge finding representations they could identify with until fairly recently. We all want to identify with the larger-than-life hero, yet we need the hero to be enough like us that we can imagine ourselves in her combat boots. The hero is the elevated aspirational fantasy of the reader. Again, the reader needs the hero.

Therefore, the reader also needs the villain. We need to see the hero face adversity, and the villain supplies it. The Joker is constantly taunting Batman, claiming they are delightfully interdependent. In fiction, the villain serves as a foil who calls the hero to action, but real life is rarely so neat and tidy. Without adversity, without moral questions, with nothing to be brave about, you remain untested. You do not have to answer tough questions or see how good you can really be. Fiction allows us to imaginatively rise up to our tallest to face the thesis of evil, become the antithesis, and reach the unknown synthesis vicariously.

Often stories are allegories of inner psychological struggles, and the villain is simply an externalized element of the reader, as is the hero. Think of the Good Kirk/Evil Kirk dichotomy in the "The Enemy Within" episode of the original *Star Trek* series, in which Captain Kirk's personality is split in two. Among other adventures, he gets into a fistfight with himself. This image is linked in my mind to a line I once heard poet Kay Ryan read: "We are no match for ourselves." Those are the best stories— a well-matched, almost separated-at-birth villain and hero make the best opponents because they reflect our internal experience.

In real-life situations from dating to politics, almost everyone thinks he or she is the "good guy" and any opposing person is the "bad guy." Few people rise above this. In fiction, the most interesting villains see themselves as heroes, and the most interesting heroes question whether they are on the correct side. Questioning oneself, rather than fervently believing in one's righteousness regardless of evidence to the contrary, can be misunderstood as weakness. Because the moral thing to do is to question oneself, this puts the real-life or fictional hero at yet another disadvantage. Being a hero isn't and shouldn't be easy.

I'm a big believer in using Joseph Campbell's story pattern of the hero's journey* as a guide when I'm writing. I see every character in my story, especially the hero and the villain, as on the journey. The difference is that the villain's achievement of his goals is perverse. He believes he is the hero of the story, but in fact he becomes the villain. He doesn't see the destructiveness of his path. He sees his path as correct and his goal as just. There are fictional villains who revel in being bad, but I would say that those writers should have looked a little deeper. Self-delusion that one's wrongdoing is justified is very human—and very villainous.

An ordinary villain is someone who can be stopped by a system that defines his actions as culpable and punishable (the criminal justice system, for example). By contrast, a supervillain controls the system or creates his own system so powerful it challenges the dominant system. Supervillains have godlike powers, and in stories without a supernatural or super-scientific element they are able to gain followers for their system, which is so powerful that it makes them into de facto gods, as cult leaders like Jim Jones were able to do.

Political and religious leaders who wield vast power and have committed large-scale crimes against humanity don't, in their own minds, set out to commit evil. On the contrary, they believe themselves to be great heroes. Hitler, Stalin, Mao, and King Leopold II† were responsible for the mass murder of millions of innocents in service to their visions. The supervillain sees no difference between what he does and what is right. Thus narcissism is the defining factor, perhaps even the core, of evil. Despite any similarities between the two archetypes, the superhero will sacrifice himself for others, whereas the supervillain will sacrifice others for himself.

In *Huntress: Year One*, I wrote this line for the hero: "On the ground, you must take sides." She invokes the memory of Dachau survivor Martin Niemoller and quotes him saying, "Neutrality helps the oppressor, never the victim." Heroes matter because they protect those who cannot protect themselves—but from whom? This is why villains are inextricable from the story. They are the catalyzing agent for the protagonists' transformation into heroes. The luxury of being a comic book reader, rather than, say, Gotham's only hope, is facing mostly internal rather than external demons. Above my desk, I posted a quote from Rumi that says, "Out beyond ideas of wrong-doing and right-doing, there is a field. I will meet you there." It's likely he wrote this after a long struggle between Good Rumi and Bad Rumi, in which he ultimately vanquished the inner villain that had, at first, kept him from finding that field.

---

* Editors' note: Campbell's plot of the hero's journey tells the story of a young, typically reluctant, hero who answers the call to adventure, separates from his family, is initiated into new wisdom, and returns to his community bearing a boon that enables the community to resolve its problems and be healed. The hero's journey metaphorically represents the transition from childhood to adulthood, from individual selfishness to selfless responsibility.

† King Leopold II of Belgium (1835–1909) founded the Congo Free State, a private colony, through which he extracted an enormous fortune through the forced labor of native Congolese in harvesting rubber. Estimates of the death toll of his brutal regime range from 5 to 15 million. He is remembered in Belgium as the "Builder King" for the grandiose development his fortune supported.

Index